STEAMING INTO HISTORY

Footplate Tales of the Last Days of Western Steam

Michael Clutterbuck

Second edition published in 2019 by Heddon Publishing.

Copyright © Michael Clutterbuck, all rights reserved.
No part of this book may be reproduced, adapted, stored in a retrieval system or transmitted by any means, electronic, photocopying, or otherwise without prior permission of the author.

ISBN 978-1-913166-03-8

Cover design by Heddon Publishing.

Cover image courtesy of Mike Poole.

This is a work of fiction. Names, characters, businesses, places, events and incidents are either the products of the author's imagination or used in a fictitious manner. Any resemblance to actual persons, living or dead, or actual events is purely coincidental.

Book design and layout by Katharine Smith, Heddon Publishing.

www.heddonpublishing.com
www.facebook.com/heddonpublishing
@PublishHeddon

This book is dedicated to my late father, William Harold Clutterbuck, himself a railwayman. In giving his son a Hornby train in 1937, he passed on a bug which still claims me firmly. My only regret is that he is no longer with us to see the results. Thank you, Dad, for all you did for us.

Introduction

This book is a sequel to *Steaming into the Firing Line*. Originally, I had no thought of writing a second set of stories. Although there were a couple of requests for a sequel made by kind reviewers of the first book, it was only when the editor felt that further details of the adventures of Lance and George might be welcome that I began to wonder whether I might find something in my Macbook if I put my mind to it. This book is the result.

The stories here deal with the situation mainly between 1946 and 1965 when steam disappeared from the Western Region. However, those wishing to know more about Lance's career in his diesel days after 1965 will have to be satisfied with Chapter 20. The Western Region was a diesel only railway from 1966 onwards until the end of its existence, and I know very little about the diesels, and had in any case migrated by this time to Australia.

The post-war decline of the railway system and its take-over by bureaucrats who demoted the railways in the UK to a second class network allow me a rich source of comment on a system of government which permits a country's rulers to radically change direction every four or five years. The failure to understand the necessity of having (and paying for) efficient public transport needing long-term planning and managed by those who know the business is still not widely appreciated. Not that the situation is necessarily different elsewhere. Here in Australia, for example, 150 years after the introduction of railways, our main routes still have three different gauges! Curiously perhaps, I have no beef with Dr Beeching; like a well-behaved bureaucrat he only did what he was told to do.

Mike Clutterbuck
Melbourne 2014

Steaming into History

Footplate Tales of the Last Days of Western Steam

1 - George considers Lance's future (September 1946) 1
2 - Aftermath of War (March 1947) 11
3 - George meets an old friend (July 1948) 20
4 - Kids! (May 1949) 29
5 - Driver Hargreaves! (November 1950) 37
6 - Lance's driving is under question (August 1951) 45
7 - Lance's narrow squeak (October 1952)......................... 54
8 - A final joint effort (January 1953).............................. 64
9 - Domestic developments (July 1954) 73
10 - The new apprentice (October 1955).......................... 82
11 - 'A snatch in time' (November 1956)......................... 91
12 - Lance gets technical (August 1957).......................... 99
13 - Lance meets a Duchess and gets political (March 1958) 108
14 - Lance meets his match (July 1959) 116
15 - *Vale!* Driver George Denton (July 1960).................... 124
16 - Wedding bells for Lance and Sally (May 1961)............ 132
17 - The Great Freeze (December 1962) 141
18 - Lance begins to run out of steam (April 1963) 149
19 - Decimation by the Doctor (October 1964)................. 157
20 - Lance reaches the BR terminus (Nov 1965 - Oct 1980). 165
The Engines i
Glossary iv

1 - George considers Lance's future
(September 1946)

Fireman Lance Hargreaves looked up from pulling coal forward on his tender while the train, a Wolverhampton to Birkenhead stopper, paused to entrain passengers at Wellington's down main platform. He heard a locomotive struggling with its parcels train as it rumbled past them on the down through line. A short parcels train should have been an easy task for a big Hall class 4-6-0, but the grime-encrusted engine was spouting steam from all sorts of orifices it shouldn't have It was clearly in need of serious attention either from shed fitters or, more likely, from the Works at Wolverhampton.

As it proceeded slowly through the station, Lance turned to his driver. "What's the bettin' we'll get held up, Mr D., with that ahead of us?"

"You could be right, Lance, just think yourself lucky that ours is in fairly good nick."

Lance and George's 43xx 2-6-0 Mogul - a mixed traffic engine - had only recently been for a 'sole and heel', as a minor maintenance check was known.

Driver George Denton was a short man but he was uncommonly clean for a steam locomotive driver; his shoes had been polished that morning, his overalls were spotless and his driver's cap gleamed. Indeed he could almost be described as dapper, but any fireman assuming that George was therefore something of a shallow dandy was rapidly disabused of such a belief.

George Denton was one of the best drivers in the whole division and there was almost no situation a GWR engine could get itself into that he couldn't handle.

George was in his late 50s and had begun his railway career some 40 years earlier, before the First World War had interrupted it. He remembered the condition of the rolling stock after the end of that war and knew it would be several years before the railways recovered from the more recent conflict. His fireman, Lance Hargreaves, had a stocky build and was strong – a useful feature for a steam locomotive fireman - and although he had left school early, Lance had a quick and ready wit which made him a highly diverting companion for Driver Denton. Indeed, George had decided that his fireman should be encouraged to go for promotion, and he had set about working on him. He had explained the negative consequences of Lance's appearance and coarse language on his prospects for promotion, and some pleasing results had been obtained. However, but George had long given up trying to improve Lance's morals; the lad was lecherous by nature, and no effort on George's part would alter that.

The parcels train had by now moved ahead but its locomotive was making such heavy weather that George knew it wouldn't be long before the crew would have to fail their engine and request a replacement, probably in Shrewsbury or Wrexham; he couldn't see it reaching Chester in its present condition.

The Great Western Railway, like the other big three railway companies, had managed its fleet through the six years of war with less than satisfactory maintenance and it was now paying the price. The government had taken over the railways for the duration of the war and, while the railways were back in private hands, there had been little compensation for the huge burden they had been forced to carry. Consequently the service provided was frequently inadequate, and railway staff had to put up with bitter complaints from the public who seemed to expect everything back to the halcyon days of pre-war travel.

Nevertheless, in some ways in life things were changing for the better. Lance shut the firebox doors, put down his shovel and turned to his driver.

"I saw me first banana yesterday, Mr D.," he said conversationally as the passengers were boarding the Birkenhead train at Wellington.

"Oh?"

"Yeah, me and me mum were –"

"My Mum and I .."

"Right; me mum and I were sitting down by the river 'avin' a picnic lunch an' a lady with a little girl – about five she must've bin - came along and sat on the next bench. The mum gave the kid a banana an' said, 'You eat that while I go an' get a bun,' and she went off."

"Did the little girl enjoy the banana?"

"No, she took a bite and put it down, pullin' a face. 'Ooh, I don't like *that!*' she ses, so I went over to 'er an' showed her that she 'ad to peel it first!"

George chuckled. "Did she like it then?"

"Did she what! That banana disappeared down 'er gullet like a – 'ere, the signal's cleared."

The guard's whistle soon sounded and his green flag waved from the rear of the train.

"We've got the green," called Lance, looking back down the

platform. His driver nodded and lifted the regulator. Their locomotive began to move off.

Not for the first time, George thought how fortunate the Great Western Railway had been to get the lad back. Two years previously Lance had been seriously injured when a V1 bomb had dropped. The explosion had put both Lance and George in hospital; Lance had almost lost a leg, but had somehow recovered and got back into the cab as an engineman.

In spite of chattering on, Lance had kept an eye on the signal and hadn't let his concentration on his duties lapse. George thought it was definitely time Lance started preparing himself for promotion. Fireman Hargreaves had been George's regular fireman for several years and George believed that the lad had the potential to be an excellent Driver. To reach this level would mean an exam and promotion first to the post of Passed Fireman, allowed to drive under supervision.

In reality, it had long been George's habit to give all his competent firemen a session on the regulator while he handled the shovel. This had the effect of giving a tired fireman a rest as well as preparing him for the responsibilities of driving. Many drivers did the same thing even though it wasn't permitted; locomotive inspectors were aware of the practice and generally turned a blind eye to it as it was regarded as unofficial training.

As Lance and George entered the Shrewsbury environs, they saw the short parcels again waiting on a siding without an engine. They rounded the curve into the station and noticed the Hall coupled to a large Prairie tank engine being towed on the Hereford line to the GWR shed at Coleham.

"Didn't think they'd get too far," commented George, "They were lucky to reach Salop. Let's hope there's a spare engine for them."
"'An let's 'ope they don't get ahead of us," added Lance, "We might be 'eld up in the platform while they pass, 'an lose time."
George looked at his fireman in approval; "You're thinking like a true engine driver, Lance. By the way, are you studying your rule book? You'll need to be thinking of your promotion to Passed Fireman before you can be a Driver."
"*Driver*, Mr D?" Lance was startled, "I'm only 26!"
"26 or not, Lance, you've been firing for ten years already and you've been doing enough driving for me to know you should be seriously thinking about your future with the Great Western. One day, you could make a competent driver."
Mustn't give the lad too much praise, thought George, *it could go to his head. But the fact remains, one day he'll make a brilliant driver - he's got the feel for it.*
"Another thing, Lance; I've three favours to ask of you."
"Yeah? Wot?"
"One: get stuck into your rule book and prepare yourself for the driver's exam."
"Okay, if you're sure."
"Two: work on improving your language. Read good books and think about your diction and vocabulary. Listen to the BBC announcers."
"No slang 'an that?"
"Nothing wrong with slang in the right place, Lance; it often expresses feelings well. But it can be misunderstood."
"Right; and the third favour?"
"We've worked together for a long time now. No more 'Mr D.' As from now, I am George to you."

This rocked Lance back on his metaphorical heels. This man was like a father figure to him; to call him 'George' was, Lance felt, bordering on disrespect. On the other hand it implied a certain familiarity which Lance thought he could be comfortable with. He nodded slowly.

"George it is, Mr D.," he said and grinned.

While they were talking, there was a loud rumbling sound as the parcels train hurried past them on the down through line; it had a big Prairie 2-6-2T tank engine at its head and George smiled when he caught sight of its driver as the engine passed them.

"I don't think the parcels will hold us up much, Lance," he said, "The driver is Dick Osbourne."

"Ah," replied Lance, "Yeah, I fired to 'im once, Mr – er - George; I reckon 'e's got shares in coalmines; 'is fireman 'as to work 'ard, but 'e certainly don't like bein' late. An' I've seen 'im getting a big Prairie to a speed it's not supposed to be able to do."

Their faith in Driver Osbourne's inclinations appeared justified, as they were not held up at all and they pulled into Chester General's bay Platform Three on time. Lance swung down from the cab to uncouple their engine; the train was reversing here and their Mogul was to go to the shed for turning and servicing before its next turn of duty.

A week or so later, the two men were crewing another 51xx 2-6-2T Prairie tank on a stopping turn from Birkenhead to Chester. This was usually fairly relaxing work, especially for the fireman because keeping enough steam pressure on the gauge for the driver was much easier than maintaining the high pressure needed for an express passenger service. As they pulled up in Hooton they saw a breakdown train in the yard. A shunter came up to them while they were waiting for the starting signal.

"There's been a derailment ahead on the up main," he told them, "You'll have about twenty minutes' time."

"Good chance to stretch my legs for a bit," said Lance, "I might even eat my sandwiches on a luxurious station seat."

He climbed down from the cab and walked along the platform before sitting down on a seat and opening his sandwich pack. He listened with increasing fascination to two Australian soldiers who met each other on the platform; one was a sergeant.

"G'day Jim," the soldier addressed the sergeant in a somewhat familiar tone, thought Lance.

"How're yer going Sam?" replied the sergeant, who didn't appear be at all put out by the informal manner of address, "How's your new corporal?"

"Ahh, 'e's fine," came the response, "In fact 'e's a bonzer bloke fer a Pom."

"The Poms aren't all bastards," commented the sergeant, who didn't seem to worry that he was surrounded by them, "And how's your new sheila?"

"She's nice," the soldier's face became animated.

"For a Pom," added the sergeant, and they both laughed.

At that moment a locomotive puffed gently past them. The sergeant pointed to it and exclaimed, "Did you know that in the war one of those engines brought down a German fighter?"

"A German *fighter*?" the soldier laughed in disbelief, "Come on Jim, yer pullin' me plonker!"

"No, fair dinkum. It was in the paper; the German fighter strafed the engine which exploded as the plane went over and it crashed."

There was a shout and a wave from Lance's cab, so he got up and joined his driver once more.

"We ready to go again, er - George?"

"Yes, we're about to get the green."

The starting signal dropped and they moved off. Lance glanced at the breakdown crew clearing up their gear as George took their Prairie past the re-railed vans on the siding.

"I was listening to a couple of Aussie squaddies on the platform; one was a sergeant but they were talking like they were mates," he said.

"Yes, I knew a few Australians in the first War," said George, "They were generally more informal than we were."

"And one of them," continued Lance, "Said he'd read about an engine that brought down a German fighter during the war. Did you ever hear about that?"

"Oh yes," answered George, "It was an 0-4-4T D3 tank engine on the Southern. The low-flying fighter strafed it and the boiler exploded as the aircraft passed overhead. Either some of the shrapnel or escaping steam from the engine must have hit something vital in the plane and it dipped and crashed."

"What about the poor bloody enginemen?"

"No-one in the cab at the time, as it happened, but the German pilot was killed."

"How do you know all these things?"

"Unlike you, young Lance, I read a proper newspaper, not your Tit-Bits rag. And if you were to read a decent paper, you'd know that the GWR will soon cease to exist."

Lance stopped shovelling and stared at George. "You what?"

"The railways are going to be nationalised."

"Nationalised?"

"Taken over by the government – just think; we'll all be civil servants!"

This was too deep for Lance, who had a practical attitude to life.

"Civil servants, eh? Bet they don't increase our pay, though."

"Now Lance," said George conversationally, "Here's an easy question for you: what's the world's fastest steam locomotive?"

"Every kid knows that, George, it's the LNER A4 *Mallard*; it did 126 mph down Essendine bank in 1938."

"Correct of course. Now a harder question; what's the second fastest?"

"You can't catch me with that; it's the LMS no. 6220 *Coronation*. She did 114 mph 'an nearly came a cropper 'ittin' the points just outside Crewe."

"Wrong, Lance, think again."

Lance was puzzled; "I was sure it was the LMS streamliner."

"No, it was a German Baltic 4-6-4 No. 05.002; and do you know what speed it reached?"

"No."

"200.04 kph."

"Er - what's that in our money?"

"125 mph."

"*125?* That's only one mile an hour slower than the LNER!"

"That's not all; did you know that another German train travelled at 126 mph in 1903?"

"You mean 126 *k*ph?"

"No; *m*ph."

"What? 26 miles an hour faster than our *City of Truro*?"

"Yes, but it wasn't a steamer; it was an electric near Berlin."

"Blimey!"

"Then they had another train which did 230.2 kph in 1931."

"Wot's that in miles per hour?"

"143 mph."

"But that's faster than *Mallard*."

"Yes, but this one wasn't a steamer either."

"Ah, electric then?"

"No, driven by a propeller."

"A *propeller?* Yer 'avin' me on!"

"Not at all, but they couldn't use it; it caused too much damage at the stations as it passed at speed."

As they passed the halt at Mollington, Lance paused in his shovelling and asked, "If the Jerries are so bloody good, 'ow come they lost two wars?"

To this George had no ready answer, but Lance did. He grinned at George.

"Yer know why, don't yer?"

"No."

"Simple," said his fireman triumphantly, "Their armies didn't 'ave enough railwaymen in 'em!"

George closed his eyes and smiled in delight. In this job, with Fireman Lancelot Hargreaves as your mate, entertainment was guaranteed.

2 - Aftermath of War (March 1947)

The short passenger train shuffled from station to station along the beautiful Welsh valley, but Lance had little time to admire the scenery. He was firing to Rob Snell of Salop shed because George Denton had a week off. Lance had technically 'learned the road', as enginemen called the familiarisation process, but he hadn't worked this line very often and he didn't remember exactly where all the signals were so had to keep a sharp lookout.

Yet the run was difficult aside from that; Rob was close to retirement and not in the best of health. He had twice had his train machine-gunned during the war, and Lance had been taken quietly aside at Salop's Coleham shed by another driver and warned that Rob's nerves had suffered because of this. The driver suggested that Lance should be extra careful to be as sensitive towards Rob as possible.

The weather was not helping either; it was hazardous. The temperature was very low for March and parts of the Central Wales line were in thick fog, requiring the occasional use of fog detonators on the line to warn of signal checks. None of this was good for Rob's mental state. Lance noticed him jump in fright every time one of the detonators on the line exploded.

They rounded a curve and to Lance's relief the fog eased off and visibility allowed them to see about 600 yards ahead. They were just beginning to relax when they heard a sudden, loud roar. A very low-flying Spitfire shot about 20 feet overhead and began a slow turn across the valley before it began to head back to them.

"Christ!" yelled Rob, "We're being attacked!"

He lifted the regulator, quickly accelerating the train beyond its permitted speed.

"It's OK, Mr Snell," called Lance, "It's only a Spitfire pilot 'avin' a game with us!"

Lance's words had no effect on the driver; Rob was in shock and continuing to accelerate the train.

"There's a tunnel ahead," he shouted to Lance, "We'll get into it and we'll be safe in there!"

"No need Mr S., the war's over," Lance patted Rob's arm, but still it made no difference. The regulator was held up and the train continued its mad rush towards the tunnel. The Spitfire roared up towards them again and Lance, furiously angry with the pilot, hurled a lump of coal up at the aircraft as it shot past them again. The lump hit the side of the fuselage and left a dent in the stressed skin of the plane. The aircraft swerved away and sped off up the valley. By now the train had entered the tunnel and Rob slammed on the brakes for an emergency stop. He looked in triumph at Lance.

"The bugger won't get us in here," he grinned, "We've foxed him!"

"If we wait a few minutes," said Lance, "He'll be gone and we can move on again."

Rob nodded. After a while, he drove the train slowly out of the tunnel, searching the sky carefully for any sign of the plane.

At Moat Lane Junction there was an inspector on the platform. He waved Rob down and asked him why the train was running behind schedule.

"We were attacked by a German fighter," asserted Rob, "We went into a tunnel to hide for a while."

The inspector stared at him.

"*A German fighter?*" he asked, startled.

"Yes," Rob assured him seriously, "You officials sit in your safe little offices while we enginemen have to drive trains under German fighters and bombers."

"German fighter," nodded the inspector, writing in his notebook. He looked back up to the cab. "Come down a moment please, Fireman Hargreaves."

Lance clambered down as the inspector turned to Rob, "Thank you Driver Snell, I need some corroboration from your fireman, then I'll let you get on."

"What the hell is your driver talking about?" the inspector asked, "Is he drunk?"

"No sir," replied Lance, "He was attacked twice in his train during the war, an' we were just buzzed by a Spitfire pilot 'avin' a bit of fun. I think it upset 'is nerves. Shook me up a bit an' all."

"Is he safe to drive, do you think?"

Lance hesitated. "I'm not sure, sir."

The inspector peered back up to the cab and said thoughtfully, "I don't like having a driver like that in charge of a train. Er - you're not a Passed Fireman are you?"

"No sir," replied Lance, "I've only bin firing about ten years."

"Hmmm," the inspector paused. "No, I don't want to take the risk. I'm going to take your driver off the train on the grounds that I consider him to be too ill to continue. That doesn't apply to you, of course. We'll find you another driver to take your train on to Aberystwyth."

A week later, Lance was called into shedmaster Tomlinson's office to discuss how a lump of coal had damaged a passing Spitfire in Central Wales.

"Er - that was me, sir," explained the fireman, "I got angry when a Spit pilot buzzed us and caused my driver to lose his nerve. I just chucked the lump of coal at him."

"Driver Snell has been pensioned off early as being unfit for driving. He has received some compensation. But the RAF are telling us that their pilot was simply flying up the valley."

"'E was buzzin' us, sir!" said Lance indignantly. "'E did it twice!"

"Yes, I believe you, Fireman Hargreaves. I doubt that anyone could throw a lump of coal high enough to hit a Spitfire in normal low flight, and I shall inform the RAF so. I shall also inform them that their pilot's 'bit of fun' has cost a blameless and experienced driver his career, and the Great Western a valuable driver, not to mention the GWR's insurance a good deal of money."

"Yes sir, er - will that be all, sir?"

Tomlinson nodded and returned to his papers. Lance turned and walked out of the office, shutting the door gently behind him. As he left, he heard a snort of laughter from behind the office door.

Talking over the incident with George Denton two weeks later, Lance explained what had happened and George sighed.

"Yes, the public have sympathy for the firemen in the Fire Brigade in the Blitz but they forget that a lot of railwaymen, as you and I know only too well, were injured or even killed through enemy action while just doing their jobs on the home front. Remember Fred Leeming who was killed in Birkenhead by some shrapnel? Rob Snell is another victim, even though his problem came after the War."

A more positive reminder of the war came a few weeks later as Lance was uncoupling his Grange class engine from the Pwllheli to Birkenhead semi-fast at Chester's Platform Three. He bent to shut off the vacuum brake and as he did so he heard a muffled ejaculation on the nearby bay. It sounded odd.

"Aua, verdammt!"

Lance looked over in surprise to see the fireman of the up Paddington at Platform Two, who had clearly been uncoupling his big Prairie 2-6-2T tank engine from the train. The man had taken his heavy glove off and was examining his thumb.

"What's up, mate?" asked Lance. He didn't recognise the fireman.

"This screw coupling is faulty; the threads are damaged and the bar dropped on my hand." The man had a strong foreign accent.

Lance went over and had a look. "Yeah, I can see the threads are worn. You'll 'ave to get the coupling replaced. I 'aven't see yer before; what shed are yer from?"

But before the fireman could answer, there was a shout from his cab. "Ingo, you having a kip or something? Get back up here!"

The driver leaned out of the cab, but when he saw who his fireman was talking to he grinned. "Hey up, young Lance, getting to know our new boy, are you? This is Fireman Ingo Meyer from Birkenhead shed."

"Ingo? What kind of a moniker's that?" Lance asked Ingo.

"It is a good German name," said Ingo with a grin. "Yes, I know; I'm a bloody Jerry!"

Lance was embarrassed. "Er - I wasn't goin' to say that!"

There was another call, this time from Lance's driver. "Lance, what's the hold up?' George leaned out and saw the two firemen. "Oh hello Ingo, how're things?"

Before the conversation could continue, the backing signal on Platform Two clanged down and Ingo said, "Sorry Lance, it is good to meet you but I must go."

He climbed back into his cab and the locomotive trundled off, following the train at a distance of several yards until it reached the end of the platform, where it halted until the signal for the shed showed clear.

"So you met our latest recruit, Lance," commented George as they waited for their backing signal to allow them out of the platform and into the shed for servicing. "I met him a couple of weeks back. He's an ex-POW. He was serving with the Afrika Korps and was captured in Libya in 1943. He heard later that his whole family had been lost in Hamburg in an air raid and on his release, he decided to stay here."

"Yeah, I heard that a few POWs liked it 'ere; but how come 'e's a fireman already? Surely 'e'd 'ave to do some cleaning' first."

"Yes, in the normal course of events, but he was a driver in Germany before the Wehrmacht conscripted him. The GWR can't promote him to Driver yet, but take it from me, they will soon; he knows his stuff."

Their backing signal dropped, George lifted the regulator gently and the Prairie moved off to slow down until the platform end signal cleared. They followed the Paddington engine across the station throat to the shed. Here they disposed of their locomotive and Lance went to have chat to Ingo while the latter was getting used to drinking tea.

It was a cold morning and Lance was glad to be in the enginemen's cabin, enjoying a quick brew while waiting for his mate.

"We've got a nasty job today, Lance," George came away from the enginemen's board looking grim. "We're on the cushions to Ruabon where we pick up a slow freight to Barmouth."

"So what's so bad about that then, George?" Lance found that he was getting used to calling his driver by his first name; even though there was over 30 years' difference between their ages.

"You obviously haven't heard the weather report for North Wales; it's not good."

"We'll be fine in a nice warm cab," said Lance with a degree of optimism.

Some hours later, as they left the warm compartment in Ruabon and saw the engine of their slow freight, Lance wondered whether his optimism had been misplaced. It was blowing a blizzard and the snow was falling horizontally. Their locomotive was an elderly ex-Cambrian 0-6-0 with an open cab - and it was working tender first.

"What was that you said about a nice warm cab, Lance?" There was a distinct bite in George's voice – unusual for him. His customary patient attitude to life's vicissitudes was absent.

"Ye gods!" muttered Lance; he had read this exclamation in one of his rare attempts to refine his vocabulary. George stared at him first then chuckled.

"What?"

"I'm so glad you're improving your language," replied George, his evil mood dissolving slightly.

Nevertheless, all too soon, they were both wondering what on Earth they had done to deserve such a dreadful duty. The tarpaulin they had stretched from the cab to the tender was totally inadequate to keep the snow out of the cab; by the time they had passed Llangollen and reached Carrog, they were frozen. George had the worst of it, as some of the controls were ice-cold and stiff. At least Lance had to shovel, which provided a modicum of exercise and generated some extra body heat. Also he had to open the firebox to put the coal in, exposing him briefly to the heat of the fire. George was a fit man in his late 50s, but he was finding the going very tough indeed and was heard to use language which Lance listened to in disbelief. George was always on at him about his language. However, he wisely chose to remain silent on the matter. There was no let-up in the weather as they passed in slow misery through Dollgellau and Machynlleth, then down the valley to the coast at Barmouth. There they gratefully left the train and headed straight for the warmth of the enginemen's cabin. It took many minutes and two scalding mugs of tea to bring some life back to the two men.

A sympathetic shedmaster rang their boss in Chester and told him they were in no fit state to run a return train, and they should stay overnight in Barmouth before taking a local passenger to Ruabon, where they could catch a connection to Chester.

"I've been in locomotive cabs, Lance, for almost 40 years," commented George when they had recovered their spirits, "And I have never been so bloody cold in my life! I sympathise with those poor brakemen in the 1850s, sitting on top of the coaches in the Russian trains in winter. Even wrapped up in fur coats they often froze to death before the journeys ended."

"Yeah," added Lance bitterly, "But you'd think that the railways would have learned something in the last 'undred years about lookin' after their railwaymen!"

It appeared the following day that at least the shedmaster had heard them, for he provided their passenger train with a small

Prairie tank engine which had an enclosed cab for their return run to Ruabon. From there they travelled on the cushions to Chester.

"After yesterday's run, I'm starting to think it's almost time for my retirement, Lance," said George, relaxing in the compartment.

Lance looked at him. "You can't do that yet, George."

"Oh? And why not?"

"You've got to get me past my driving test."

"Of course," nodded George, "I hadn't forgotten about that. I wasn't planning to leave straight away! I'll tell the missus she'll have to wait for that trip round the world."

For once, George had the last word.

3 - George meets an old friend (July 1948)

George was puzzled; there was something odd about his fireman but he couldn't put his finger on exactly what it was. Lance had recently succeeded in his exam and was now a Passed Fireman. He was not yet officially a Driver, but was allowed to drive under certain circumstances. The promotion to the right hand side of the cab gave most men an air of authority, a few of whom regrettably understood this as permission to bully their own fireman. This was definitely not in Lance's character, but George had noticed a slight change in him over the months since his promotion. Lance had never been short of self-confidence, and his re-classification to Passed Fireman had not altered that. No, it was something else; and the fact that he couldn't put his finger on it annoyed George. Lance and George were working a short fitted freight from Leeds to South Wales; they had taken the train on at Warrington and would leave it in the hands of a Cardiff crew at Hereford. They had been fortunate with their locomotive; not only had it been newly repaired but the Mogul 2-6-0 had even been given a new paint job and was now a gleaming black with the brand new 'British Railways' insignia on the tender. It was handling the freight with little effort, thus giving Lance an easy time with the shovel.
"I'm pleased you studied your rule book so effectively, Passed Fireman Hargreaves," commented George, "Look where it's got you."
"Yes, it was worth all the hours of all that readin' - reading," replied Lance, leaning on the shovel, "And that's not all I've bin – been - reading… Mum gave me a book by Jane Austen to study."

George had been noting the time of passing Ludlow in his notebook but he paused; the penny dropped. That's what it was! Lance was improving his language skills. Not before time either, thought George.

"Sounds like you've been paying close attention too, Lance," said George. Then something else occurred to him. "Have you been taking some kind of lessons?"

"Yes, that's right. Once a week for six months."

"I bet your tutor was an attractive young female!"

Lance shrugged. "So what, George?"

"I knew it," George was amused. "I wonder if you will ever change, Lance?"

Lance's mind flicked back to his first lesson with the tutor; indeed, 'attractive young female' was an accurate description but it missed out that although her sweater was very nicely filled, she was also a good deal more forthright than he had expected. Halfway through the lesson, she had stopped abruptly.

"Lance Hargreaves, you have a lustful expression on your face. If you want me to grab your dick, I will; but only to tie a very tight knot in it! Now; we were discussing the use of suitable adjectives."

The mental image had made Lance instantly snap his thighs together.

"Suitable adjectives," said Lance pensively.

"Suitable adjectives?" queried George, bringing him back to reality. "What the devil are you talking about? Well never mind, now that you can drive officially, you'd better get some more practice in. And as for me," here George patted his middle, "I'll practise reducing my waistline; hand me that shovel."

Lance took over the driving and George opened the firebox flaps, checking that the fire was burning satisfactorily. He then checked the gauge glass. He checked the signals as they passed through Leominster and then put four or five more shovels full of coal down the left hand side of the firebox, where a hole in the fire had appeared. George glanced unobtrusively over to the driver's side of the cab at Lance, but the latter was clearly quite comfortable, and, as far as George could see, also quite relaxed. Just then the gauge glass shattered.

"Come on Fireman Denton, don't bugger about; get it changed!" said Lance sharply with a grin on his face. "There's a spare in me - my bag."

George chuckled as he set about putting a new glass in. "Very unwise that tone of yours, Passed Fireman Hargreaves, very unwise. I'll remember it tomorrow when I'm driving back to Chester. You won't forget it either when you're firing!"

At Hereford they left their engine to a South Wales crew. Lance went to the enginemen's hostel and George left to catch up with an old friend in the city. Lance settled his bag in his bunk and cleaned himself up before going out for a pint at a nearby pub. He cast his eye over the various girls but only one of them attracted his attention. She was sitting alone at the bar and Lance stood up to walk over to her, but as he did so a young man returned to her side. He was built in a manner which suggested that he could look after himself, and Lance decided that caution rather than boldness might be wiser. He had once tried to chat up another pretty girl on a Shrewsbury train and only swift action by George had saved him from a probable spell in hospital.

Lance sighed and finished his drink. *Well I'm tired tonight anyway*, he thought to himself and went back to a lonely bed in the hostel.

Reporting to the Hereford shedmaster next morning, he was surprised to find that George was absent.

"Bit of an emergency this morning, Hargreaves," said the shedmaster to him, "Your driver had to take a light engine urgently to Leominster. I know you're a Passed Fireman and want you to take a Salop stopper and pick him up on the way. I'll give you our Fireman Evans for the run. You can leave Evans at Leominster and he can make his own way back."

Lance nodded and walked over to the engine; this was a large Prairie 2-6-2T, and Lance pulled a face when he saw it. It was already a warm day and the enclosed cab of the Prairie would quickly get unpleasantly hot. The fireman was already there and getting the fire set to his satisfaction. Lance introduced himself. The fireman shook his hand, naming himself as Gwynne Evans. They backed onto their train at the station and waited for the guard's green flag. Fireman Evans looked back down the train and then called out, "We've got the green."

Lance lifted the regulator and they moved off slowly.

The run was uneventful and Lance was impressed by the young man's handling of his job. "How old are you, Gwynne?" he asked.

"24," replied Gwynne, "Why?"

"Just wondered," said Lance, "You seem to be a bit young to be a fireman already. Yet you can obviously manage a shovel."

"I was in the Great Western as a cleaner for a while, but was useless in the job and left to join the army. I was demobbed in '46 and decided to try again."

"What did you do in the army?"

"I was trained as a sniper and did a bit of unarmed combat."

"Sounds dangerous."

"Aye, well you quickly learn to deal with tricky situations."

"So what made you want to come back into the railway?"

"There was this bloke, Driver Denton; in spite of my many cock ups he tried hard to help me, and…"

"Not George Denton?" said Lance in surprise.

Gwynne smiled. "Yes, I think that was his name. Do you know him?"

Lance nodded. "I've met him," he replied and smiled inwardly as a thought occurred to him.

"After my demob," Gwynne continued, "I thought again about the railway and decided to give it another go. I wanted to show Driver Denton, if he's still driving that is, that his hard work might have paid off. I think in hindsight that I was just lacking in confidence; I actually like the idea of one day driving a steam locomotive."

"I'm sure he'd appreciate knowing about your interest."

While they were chatting, Lance noticed that young Evans' eyes never stopped checking the gauges, and he peered into the firebox from time-to-time, placing a few shovels full of coal around the fire where they were needed. Gwynne's aim in the shaking and rattling cab was accurate and he didn't spill much on the cab floor.

It was clear too that Fireman Evans knew the road well; he called out the signals in good time for Lance to react if they had to slow or stop.

"Fireman Hargreaves, you're a Salop man, I understand?"

"No, I'm from Chester," Lance paused, "Like Driver Denton. He's still driving, by the way."

"Chester? That's where I started as a cleaner during the war. Look, would you do me a great favour and pass on my best wishes – and thanks - next time you see Driver Denton?"

Lance turned his face away so that Gwynne Evans couldn't see his grin. "Yes, I'l. do that for you. I'll probably be seeing him again before long."

Lance noticed a ganger ahead of them waving a red flag, and a group of workmen on the track a few hundred yards beyond. He saw the gang foremen blow a horn although, of course, he couldn't hear it. The workmen hurriedly stepped aside as the train neared. "What are they doing here?" asked Lance, "I didn't see any notice about work on the track here anywhere."

Gwynne Evans shook his head. "There was nothing about it this morning. I checked carefully. Must be something the linesman reported only today."

Lance slowed the train down to about 15 miles per hour, as far as he could judge; only the big express passenger engines had speedometers, so other drivers had to use their judgement. The track where the workmen had been working was very rough. The ballast had been shovelled away and the sleepers exposed. Clearly something out of the ordinary had happened as this wasn't a normal re-ballasting exercise; trackwork of that nature was planned well in advance and enginemen were given plenty of warning.

Even at the slow speed they were travelling, the ride was very rough and Gwynne surveyed the cab floor where a few bits of coal had been shaken out of the bunker hole.

"We'll be in Leominster in 15 minutes, and I can start to clean up for the next fireman," muttered Gwynne.

"Don't worry about it, Gwynne," grinned Lance, "I'll be sure to inform the next fireman why the floor isn't spotless. I know he won't mind. You've left him a good fire to work with."

"Thanks, Mr Hargreaves, but it's my job to ensure that my replacement has a clean cab; I don't like getting into a dirty cab myself, so I don't want to do the same to another crewman."

"Very laudable," commented Lance, thinking to himself, Crikey, I'm even sounding like George now. 'Laudable' was a word he had heard from his driver on occasions.

Gwynne shovelled up the remaining larger pieces of coal and threw them into the firebox, he then took out the coal-watering pipe and began to hose down the cab floor. Lance sat on the wooden tip-up shelf which passed for a seat, designed without enginemen's comfort in mind, and lifted his feet to avoid them getting soaked. Soon the cab was spotless again. They were approaching Leominster and Lance wondered how he could remove Gwynne from the cab for a few moments while George climbed in.

"Gwynne," he said, "Do me a favour. Nip out and check the right-hand cylinder cover for me when we stop. We've been losing a bit of steam; I tightened a loose bolt in there this morning and it needs to be checked to make sure it's still tight."

Gwynne nodded and moved to the driver's side of the cab behind Lance as the engine came to a gentle stop. He climbed down the steps and went to examine the cylinder cover. Meanwhile George Denton, who had been waiting on the platform, climbed up, glanced briefly into the firebox and gazed around the clean cab.

"You've got a good fireman here, Lance," he said approvingly. "You've organised him well."

"Not me, George, he's done all this off his own bat. He certainly knows his stuff."

"Nothing wrong that I could see, Mr Hargreaves." The voice came from outside as Gwynne climbed back into the cab. Then he caught sight of George.

"Mr Denton!" he cried in astonishment, "What're you doing here?"

George was equally surprised. "Gwynne Evans! I thought you'd given up the railway life after your time in Chester. The last I heard, you were busy sniping at German soldiers. What brought you back?"

Gwynne paused, considering his reply. "I suppose I could say that you did. I actually enjoyed much of my railway time, but was always frightened of making mistakes. Then I had a sergeant in the army who taught me confidence. I remembered how you tried to encourage me, so I tried the railways again. And here I am, thanks to you."

The guard's whistle interrupted the discussion and, after exchanging addresses with George, Gwynne hurriedly left the cab. Lance took up the shovel once more and George moved to take up the regulator. On their way to Shrewsbury, George explained how Gwynne, as a cleaner, had been very nervous at almost every job he tried. Lance assured him that while that may have been true at the time, Gwynne now had the makings of a very competent engineman.

"Well, I have to say, I'm surprised," said George as he slowed down for the stop at Ludlow, "I never expected to see him as a railwayman, he was almost dangerous in his work in the cab in those days. I'm very pleased he's doing so well."

George was caught by Lance's next question. "Do you know, George, what you're going to do in your retirement in – what - four years?"

"My retirement? Well no, to be honest. I haven't given the matter much thought. Why on Earth are you asking that?"

"Consider this, George; you take an uncouth slob like me and convert him into a Passed Fireman – mind you, it's taken you a

dozen years - then you get a clumsy cleaner and turn him into a Fireman in four years. You could apply to the Western Region to train useless buggers into decent enginemen!"
George shook his head, smiling.

4 - Kids! (May 1949)

Driver Albert Lansdowne was depressed; he looked at the six coaches from the Wrexham train sitting at Platform Two at Chester's Northgate Station and sighed. He was reminded of the minister's sermon on the previous Sunday based on the text of 'How are the mighty fallen'.

Could apply to me, he considered, *here I am in an unimportant and ancient tank engine, shunting a rake of local coaches, when I should be taking a B12 on a Marylebone express. All because of one stupid mistake.*

Albert had been a top link driver based in Sheffield, taking expresses to Liverpool and London, when he had taken his train at 65 mph just south of Leicester through a 20 mph speed restriction. He had read the daily notices, he remembered, but had clean forgotten the restriction.

He had to acknowledge that the demotion to local work at Chester Northgate could have been far worse; he was lucky to be able to continue driving at all; this hadn't been the first time he'd missed a speed restriction, but it had been the most dangerous. An error of that nature could have had catastrophic results and could have led to instant dismissal, but his driving record was otherwise good. Albert had joined the Great Central Railway as a cleaner in 1910, and had been driving since 1931. He privately admitted to himself too that his eyesight was no longer what it had been, and the doctor who conducted the regular driver's check-up had warned him that he might have to give up driving in a year or two, even though he was only 54.

Fireman Denis Bolton had already uncoupled and Albert moved the engine forward to the release crossover before backing slowly past the coaches. Denis swung himself up onto the cab steps and hung on there, waiting until Albert could cross back to the down line and couple up again. Northgate station was cramped and the carriages were often stabled in the bay platform at Liverpool Road station only half a mile away around the sharp curve.

Liverpool Road station was a curiosity; it was generously laid out with four through platforms plus a bay. Platforms One and Two were used for the Wrexham line from the nearby Northgate terminus, although it was rare that any passengers got on or off. Platforms Three and Four were on the through tracks from Northwich and Manchester to Birkenhead and Wrexham, yet Albert had never seen a passenger train using them. The tracks were used for heavy freight trains to the John Summers steelworks at Shotton and to Birkenhead docks. There was a small yard with a siding or two, but little business was carried out there.

Denis, having coupled the C13 4-4-2T tank engine to the coaches, clambered back into the cab and they waited for the platform starter signal to allow them to proceed. They then drew the coaches back round the sharp, steep curve, under the bridge, and clear through Liverpool Road station to the station throat, where they could then back the coaches into the bay. All very humdrum until they reached the crossover which was to take them into the bay platform; then there was a shake from the train.

"Christ, look at that!" shouted Denis, staring back at the coaches as they pushed them back into the platform. Albert quickly spun around in time to catch a glimpse of one of the coaches swaying vigorously before settling down sedately once more. He applied the brakes instantly and the train came to a standstill.

"Get down, Den, and have a quick butcher's," called Albert, screwing down the locomotive handbrake. Denis dropped down and walked along the train, looking at the wheels. Nothing appeared to be amiss, but he walked back, checking once more before climbing back into the cab.

"Nothing obvious Bert," he said, "We're still on the road."

"Well something happened," replied Albert, "That bloody coach nearly tipped over. I'll go and have a look myself."

With that, he climbed down from the cab and walked along the track, staring underneath all the coaches as he went. He climbed back into the cab, shaking his head in disbelief.

"Buggered if I can see anything either," he told his fireman, "Let's check again. You go along one side and I'll go on the other. One of us should be able to see something, otherwise we'll have to call the station and that'll cause no end of paperwork."

Denis nodded. He too was not enamoured with the thought of the amount of paperwork the incident could generate for them if they had been in any way remiss. He glanced out of the cab, sighing, and stiffened.

"Half a mo," he said, "Something doesn't look right."

"What?"

"Look at the points just there in front of us."

Albert looked, "What about them?"

"There's something different about them."

Albert looked again, "I can't see anythi..? Hey, you're right, Den; there is something. What's that sticking up right on the vee?"

They both got down and walked over to the points to get a closer look. Albert bent down and pulled up a large piece of metal jammed into the vee of the crossing. It was a huge metal washer about five inches in diameter.

"How the hell did that get there?" they stared at each other. As they stood there, they heard a laugh and a sudden scuffle in the hedge about 20 yards away, and as they looked up they saw two lads haring off down the embankment.

"Little bastards!" snarled Albert, "Their trick could have derailed the whole train. We'd better report this quickly."

They reported the matter to the stationmaster, who phoned Northgate station. An inspector was sent down and he was interviewing the two enginemen when a police sergeant arrived on his bike.

The stationmaster told the sergeant that the station area had not been fenced off for years, if ever, and that kids often pottered around the yard; indeed one or two schoolboys from a local preparatory school were regulars on the morning and afternoon local to Blacon.

"Well I didn't see the kids in any uniform," said Albert, "Did you, Den?"

"No, these were scruffy little devils," said Denis, "But I reckon I'd know them again."

The inspector made a note or two, as did the police sergeant. Then he turned to the enginemen and said, "Look you two, could you keep an eye open for the next few days? You never know, the little sods might try something again."

"Yes," concurred the sergeant, "And I'll tell my constables to check from time-to-time. Coppers hanging around tend to discourage kids who have mischief on their minds."

Two weeks later, Albert nudged Denis quietly as they were shunting the coaches in to the Liverpool Street bay platform again.

"Look over there, Den, there's a couple of lads sitting watching us."

Denis glanced over to where his driver was pointing. He frowned and said, "They're not making any effort to hide, the saucy little blighters."

"They don't look like the two we saw last week, though."

As Albert climbed down from the cab, the two boys stood up. They were wearing school uniforms and both had notebooks in their hands. They waited while the driver walked up to them.

"What are you lads up to?" asked Albert.

The taller boy held up his notebook and said, "John here says your engine's a D11, but I think it's a C13. Which of us is right?"

Meanwhile, Denis had joined Albert, and he looked carefully at the boys, who showed no apprehension at this inspection. Denis looked at Albert and shook his head.

"Our engine's a C13; the D11 has a tender and it's a 4-4-0."

"There!" said the taller boy to his friend, "I told you so."

"Tell me," said Albert to both boys, "Have you ever seen other boys mucking about here?"

"Yes!" The smaller boy spoke angrily, "There were two here a few days ago. We were sitting watching your coaches coming in and they told us to go away."

"What exactly did they say?" asked Denis.

Both boys remained silent.

"Come on," encouraged Albert, "What were their words?"

The boys shuffled their feet in embarrassment but refused to respond.

Denis looked at Albert, "Might have to talk to that police sergeant, Albert."

The tall boy sighed and said with obvious reluctance, "They were bigger than us and one of them said, 'Piss off you two or we'll fucking bash you!'"

Denis looked quickly away to hide his grin, while Albert tried to look shocked.

"Have you seen them since?"

"No, sir."

Denis pointed to the station building. "If you see them again," he said, "you must go straight to that building and tell the clerk there, and he'll get the police."

The boys nodded eagerly. "Yes, we'll do that."

The following day, Albert and Denis were on a Manchester Central train and were discussing the 'youth of today', as Albert called them. The D11 Director class 4-4-0 was running well and Denis could relax between the Mickle Trafford junction and Delamere. Four young lads got out at Delamere and Albert, looking at their rucksacks, said, "What's the betting they're going to camp in Delamere Forest?"

Denis agreed, "Yep, done that myself as a youngster more than once. It's a great place for a bit of camping, provided you're careful."

"Careful?" queried Albert, who was not the outdoor sort. His idea of the perfect holiday week required a B&B with a comfy armchair, three or four good crime novels, a pub and a cinema across the road for evening variety. Preferably on a road full of shops to keep his wife entertained as well. A sea front was a bonus due to his wife's belief that the fresh air did him good and got rid of 'all that steam and smoke' in his system.

"No lighting huge camp fires you can't put out; strong walking shoes; good binoculars if you have any; and no leaving papers and mess when you move on. Those kids who put that washer on the line the other day would have been a menace as campers in my view."

They had a longer pause at Altrincham where many passengers alighted to catch the electric connection to Manchester London Road. At the end of the platform stood three young boys with notebooks.

"What are they looking for?" wondered Denis, "There's not much variety of stock here."

"Are you watching for the guard's flag?" Albert reminded him.

"Oh, yes," and Denis looked back for the flag, saw it, and called to his driver, "We've got the right away, Bert."

Albert lifted the regulator and the train began to move off, but just as Denis was about to pull his head back into the cab, he glimpsed one of the young boys dart down the sloping end of the platform and put something on the track, just in front of the approaching engine.

"Albert; brake!" shouted Denis urgently, "There's a kid on the line!"

Albert slammed on the train brake with one hand and closed the regulator as Denis closed the loco steam brake and the train lurched to a sudden halt. Albert dropped from the cab and saw the train guard climbing quickly out of his van and hurrying down the platform. Enquiring heads were poking out from the windows too to see why they had stopped. Denis ran to where he had seen the boys, but they had crossed the tracks, run up the down platform and disappeared. He examined the track and picked up an item which he brought back to show the guard and his driver. It was a ha'penny.

"Little bastards; look at this," he held it up to the guard, who nodded.

"Aye, trying to make pennies out of ha'pennies," the guard said. "I'll have to make a note of this; I can't see us getting anywhere though. The little buggers have long gone."

He went back to the guard's compartment in the last coach. Denis showed the coin to Albert, who nodded.

"Yeah, seen it before," he said, then in a quieter voice added, "I must admit to having done it meself as a kid; bloody dangerous though."

Then he chuckled suddenly.

"What's so funny?" asked Denis.

"It's something I once heard from a father of three boys," said Albert, "He was a driver in Sheffield and he was once asked how he would define a boy."

"What did he say?"

"He replied that a boy was a creature bent on self destruction!"

They both laughed.

"Your mate knew what he was talking about, I've done some funny things as well in my younger days," commented Denis.

"What things, f'r instance?"

"Never you bloody mind," said Denis and he bent to shovel more coal into the firebox.

5 - Driver Hargreaves! (November 1950)

George Denton walked, scowling, into the enginemen's cabin, looking for his fireman. He saw him chatting to 'Fancy' Panton, and stalked over.

"I only go on leave for a week and you go and team up with another driver!" he said, "What's the big idea?"

"Wrong, George," said Lance with a grin, "I haven't teamed up with another driver."

"Well why am I with Fancy here on the Wolverhampton?" replied George. "That's the train you and I run. So who're you with today?"

"I'm off to Birkenhead, back to Hooton, and then West Kirby, returning to Chester, with Jackie Tonks."

George frowned. "But Jackie's a fireman; even as a Passed Fireman you can't drive with another fireman!"

Fancy smiled at Lance. "'E don't know yet, do 'e?"

"Don't know *what*?" George was getting frustrated.

"On the first day of your holiday Mr Tomlinson called me in and told me I was to take the Driver's test two days later, so I did. And I passed, thanks to your coaching."

A grin of delight lit up George's face. "That's marvellous, Lance! Driver Hargreaves! Now I can retire happy! I feel as if my life's ambition is fulfilled. I'll tell Alice to plan for that long holiday we've talked about. But this evening you and I must celebrate over a whisky or two at the Wheatsheaf before you go home to your mum."

There was a distinct spring in George's step as he and Fancy went to find their engine.

By the time they had reached Hooton, halfway to Birkenhead, Jackie Tonks put down his shovel in annoyance and turned to Lance.

"Listen, mate," he said poking his own chest with his forefinger, "Me - fireman, you – driver. Now stop checking my fire and concentrate on your driving!"

Lance grunted, embarrassed. He knew he was in the wrong; Jackie was an experienced and competent fireman and both of them knew it.

Their Prairie tank engine appeared to be in reasonable condition and they took it light engine to Hooton where they backed on to the coaches of the West Kirby train. The run to West Kirby through the pretty Wirral peninsula was straightforward with no problem sections. As they paused in Parkgate to pick up a few passengers wanting to do their shopping in West Kirby, Jackie pointed to the River Dee estuary with its wide mud flats and distant river.

"Did you know that the mayor of Chester is also the Admiral of the Dee?"

"The Admiral of the Dee? What are you talking about? Chester isn't a port, it's inland!"

"It only ceased being a port in 1948; centuries ago it was the second biggest port, after Bristol, in the west; most of the shipping to Ireland went from Chester. Cromwell took his armies from Chester to Ireland. But when the Dee began to silt up, the shipping transferred to Liverpool."

Lance stared at Jackie doubtfully. "How do you know all this?"

Jackie shrugged. "I like a bit of history; I enjoyed it at school and when I have some spare time I go down to the City Library in St John Street. How do you think Watergate Street got its name?"

"How?"

"It was the street leading to the port in Roman times."

"OK Smart Alec," said Lance and he pointed to Parkgate. "What can you tell me about Parkgate?"

"Nice day out with the wife and kids. We catch the bus from Delamere Street and spend the day walking along the riverbank, eating shrimps and cockles and watching the birds."

"The birds?" Lance's eyes lit up.

"Waterfowl, you randy bugger!" laughed Jackie. "The kids bring their bird recognition books and see what they can observe."

Good humour, it seemed, had been restored.

The weather turned the day from cold and sunny to drizzly with occasional downpours, which made Lance and Jackie thankful they were in the enclosed cab of a big tank engine. They returned with their train to Hooton and left the coaches to run light engine back to Woodside where they left their Prairie. They picked up a 43 class 2-6-0 Mogul for their next train; a semi-fast to Barmouth which they were to crew as far as Chester. It was immediately clear that their Mogul was in need of some attention.

By the time they reached Rock Ferry, where the Mersey Railway passengers from Liverpool were waiting, Lance was peering into the fire again and beginning to anger Jackie once more, who glared at him. The previous good humour appeared to have dissipated somewhat.

The next stop was Hooton and the engine was steaming poorly, even though Lance could not see anything in his glances into Jackie's fire that he would have done differently. But these glances into the fire - technically the right of any driver - were continuing to annoy Jackie. As they were passing Capenhurst he jammed his shovel into the coal in the tender and turned to face Lance.

"For Christ's sake Lance, stop bloody checking on my firing! I'm not some sprog fireman learning the job; I've 12 years' firing and know what to do as well as you do. Now pull your finger out and do your own job, not mine!"

With an effort, Lance controlled his temper; he was in charge and firemen were not supposed to get stuck into their drivers like this. On the other hand, Lance admitted to himself that he had been unnecessarily heavy handed with a man – and a friend - who was manifestly very competent (furthermore a man whose shoulders indicated an ability to handle himself firmly in the case of any physical aggression).

Lance nodded in apology. "Sorry Jackie, forgot myself again."

Going off shift, they parted in a more conciliatory frame of mind.

"How are you enjoying your driving, Lance?" George asked a week or so after his return from leave.

"Fine, George, I'm getting used to it," Lance replied.

"It's not all beer and skittles, is it?" said George with a knowing look. "I saw Jackie Tonks come off shift with you a couple of weeks back. He didn't look happy."

"Jackie's OK," said Lance, "What's he been saying to you?"

"Nothing at all," replied George, "I haven't spoken to him, but I hope you didn't try to tell him how to do his job; he's a good fireman and will make a very good driver one day."

"Well we did have a word or two but it's sorted now."

"I'm very glad to hear it," commented George as he left to find his fireman.

Just before Christmas, Lance was called in to Barry Tomlinson's office.

"You have been driving for three weeks now, Driver Hargreaves, how are you finding the job?" asked the shedmaster.

"I've spent some time on the right hand side of the cab, sir, before with Driver Denton who has often let me drive, so I am finding my feet fairly quickly, I think."

"Hmm," the shedmaster paused for a moment before continuing, "You have driven with several firemen in the few weeks you have been driving and I believe it's time you had a regular. As from tomorrow you will have Fireman Cardew. After a month or so we will review the situation. Cardew is a new man who has just come to us from Reading where he was recently a Passed Cleaner. The Reading shedmaster tells me Cardew knows his stuff, but you will need to keep an eye on him all the same. That's all."

"Yessir."

Lance nodded and went out to find someone who might give him more information about Fireman Cardew. In the enginemen's cabin he found a young fellow he didn't know.

"You Fireman Cardew, by any chance?" he asked him.

"Yessir, that's me."

"Lance Hargreaves," Lance held out his hand, adding, "I'm your driver; and don't call me 'sir', I'm Lance."

"Right – er, Lance."

"We're on the Salop stopper today, couple of trips there and back; so let's get busy. Got all your gear?"

"Yes, it's all here."

"By the way, what's your first name?"

"Geoff."

"Righto Geoff; up an' at 'em."

They walked out of the cabin to find their locomotive; it was a 4-6-0 Hall class. Geoff looked at it, puzzled.

"What's the matter, Geoff?"

"It's a modified Hall – they're good engines, a bit stronger than the regular Halls, and I would have expected a big Prairie or a 43 Mogul for the eight coaches of a Salop stopper."

Lance looked at his young fireman with approval. "I like a bloke who's thinking about his work. But have a look under the footplate just in front of the cylinders."

Geoff looked carefully and then he spotted what Lance was referring to. "Ah! 'SALOP'," he read; the home shed code was painted there. "It's working back to its home shed?"

Lance nodded, satisfied.

"Spot on, mate. Now," he added, "Can you tell me anything else about this engine?"

Geoff studied the engine carefully. "It's very clean, so it's either been recently soled and heeled, or the Salop shedmaster is very fussy about sending his engines out clean."

"Very good!"

"I don't like the paint scheme though."

"The black with the fancy lining?"

"Yes, and the number plate with the red background. That says LNWR to me. I much preferred the old GWR colours myself."

Lance was impressed.

"I didn't know that; I wondered where BR got the colour scheme from. Now, well let's take this black engine back to Salop where it belongs."

They climbed into the cab and Geoff began to work on the fire to get it into condition for the work ahead. He checked the various gauges, while Lance went round the motion with the oil can. When Lance was satisfied, he whistled to indicate readiness to depart, and the signalman set the points and signals for them to drive out of the shed. They backed on to their coaches in Number Two bay platform.

"How long have you been a Fireman?" Lance wanted to know.

"Two months; I passed my exam in Reading before I transferred up here."

Geoff leaned out of the cab, looking back along the platform to see when the guard would wave his green flag. The platform starter signal dropped. Lance was leaning out of his side of the cab, engrossed in watching a girl bending down on Platform Three, but he had his hand on the regulator and lifted it gently as Geoff called out that the guard had given them the all clear to go.

The big locomotive began to glide forward and Lance commented, "Nice bum on that girl." as the engine left the cover of the platform awning.

"Bit of sand please, Geoff," he requested as they encountered the heavy rain.

Dry sand blown from the engine's sandboxes onto the rails helped a locomotive's wheels to grip the greasy metal. The Hall gripped the rails without slipping as Geoff worked the sandboxes but he noted that Lance had responded to the weather without apparent thought, and there was no wheel spin.

The train picked up speed down the grade from Saltney, before slowing down to stop at Balderton.

"We killed a bloke here a few years back," muttered Lance. "We were running an express and the silly bugger climbed over the crossing gates to cross the line. Neither my driver or I saw him; not that it would have made any difference if we had. We were doing about 70 at the time. Now you'll have to bend your back a bit here, the next sections are steep up to Wrexham."

Arriving at Wrexham, Lance glanced into the fire and nodded; his young fireman had things under control. Then he had a thought and smiled to himself.
Between Wrexham and Ruabon, he picked up a big spanner from the tender toolbox and held it up in front of the water gauge glass. "What would you do, Geoff, if I belted the glass with this spanner?" he asked.
Geoff promptly turned to his toolbox and took out another glass, saying, "First I'd check that the fire would be OK for a couple of minutes, then I'd put this in. Three months back in Reading a gauge glass actually broke on me. That's how I know what to do; it scared the pants off me!"
"Oh," he added, "Don't try and tell me to throw the coal far enough down to ring the bell in the firebox of a King. I know that one too!"
Lance laughed. "Cocky young sod!"
Geoff is not going to be an easy tease, thought Lance. He'd have to think more about this one.

6 - Lance's driving is under question (August 1951)

Lance and his young fireman, Geoffrey Cardew, were waiting to relieve the Phwlleli to Birkenhead passenger at Corwen.
Fireman Cardew was pleased to be firing to Driver Hargreaves, who was thought to be one of the most promising young drivers in Chester's Western Region shed; he had only been promoted to driver the previous year but had been firing for twelve years before that, working his way up from Passed Cleaner to Fireman and then to Passed Fireman. Geoffrey knew that George Denton had a high opinion of Driver Hargreaves and George was widely acknowledged to be one of the finest drivers in the whole Wolverhampton Division. His opinion was respected.
Geoff had only fired once or twice to Lance before and was hoping to learn much from the man. In the run to Corwen, Lance had been totally relaxed and master of the old 43 class 2-6-0 mixed traffic locomotive, which had admittedly just returned from a major repair in Swincon and was not expected to have any steaming issues. Nevertheless, the young fireman was impressed with his driver, who made everything look so simple.
The excursion train to Pwhlleli was heavily loaded with passengers heading for their summer holidays at the Welsh coastal resorts. Its load had been strengthened by two extra coaches and it left Chester with eight.
Lance and Geoff left their train at Corwen, handing over to the Welsh crew who were taking it on to Pwhlleli. While waiting for their return train, they discussed the rumours concerning the state

of the king's health; it was reported in the newspapers to be 'of concern'.

"One of his doctors was apparently telling him to give up smoking," commented Geoff.

"Might not be a bad idea," replied Lance, "I used to smoke but gave it away and felt better afterwards."

"Anythin' else you want to give up?" asked Geoff mischievously. Like most of the Chester shed's enginemen, he was well aware of Lance's fondness for the fairer sex.

"You just watch your lip, you cheeky young sod," responded Lance, grinning, "You don't know what you're missing."

Their return train came into sight and Lance groaned when he saw the locomotive.

"Oh it's a flamin' Manor! This might be a tough ride."

"Why, Lance?" asked his fireman, "What's wrong with Manors? I've never fired one before."

"They were introduced in '38 and we were told they were an improvement on the old 43s which struggled with the heavier trains; but when we got 'em, they bloody weren't any better. They need firm handling, and even then they won't pull. You'll need to bend your back for this ride, Geoff. An' you watch the crew's faces when they get off; they'll be grinning and glad to be off her."

It was obvious to his fireman that Lance was not in a good mood.

"Well the engine looks nice and clean anyway," remarked Geoff.

"A clean engine means nothing," grumbled Lance, "It just means that some shed foreman has put the mockers on the cleaners. Now if it 'ad been repainted, that means it's been through the Works and they might have fixed a few clanks and bangs in the motion."

Sure enough, as the train came to a stop, the cabin crew were visible, preparing to climb down. They did, as Lance had predicted, have smiles on their faces.

"See what I mean?" muttered Lance, "They're happy to be out of that cab."

"She's all your, Lance me lad," said the grinning driver, "An' you're in for a surprise."

"What surprise?"

"You'll see!"

Lance and Geoff climbed into the cab and stowed their lunch boxes safely. Geoff poked his shovel in the firebox and angled it so that he could check around the fire.

"Fire seems in order," he commented then, hearing the guard's whistle, he looked back along the train and called to Lance, "We've got the green."

Lance lifted the regulator savagely and the locomotive jerked and jolted its seven coaches into motion.

Geoff was still checking down the platform and was very nearly thrown out of the cab but managed to grab hold of the side rail and clung on for dear life.

"What the hell are you doing?" he yelled at his driver, all respect abandoned.

"Godalmighty!" exclaimed Lance as he too almost fell backwards and had to clutch the regulator tightly to keep his balance.

At Llangollen, their next stop, two passengers came up to the cab, one of them shouting, "I'm off this bloody train with its half-witted driver! I'm catching the bus to Chester; it's safer!"

There were other heads leaning out of compartments along the train, many expressing identical views.

Lance frowned as they took the track towards Ruabon.

"Hmm," he murmured, "We appear to be lucky; this engine is pulling well."

They stopped at Ruabon, where they joined the main line north to Birkenhead. There, Lance pushed the engine harder as they headed towards Wrexham, and it responded with gratifying effort. Running down Gresford bank with its train and across the Dee plain at speed, Lance found himself exhilarated by the ease at which the engine was managing its load.

"How's the firing going, Geoff?" he asked.

"Much easier than you led me to believe, Lance," replied the fireman, "You said we'd be in trouble, but this Manor is handling the train like it was a Hall or a Grange."

Lance nodded, "Yep, we've got a good 'un here. This Manor's been dealt with by someone who knows what he's doin'."

As they drew in to Chester's Platform Three, they saw a locomotive inspector waiting by the buffer stops. They pulled up and he walked over to them, climbing into the cab. He stared at Lance.

"Driver Hargreaves," he began, "I was led to believe that you were a competent driver. However, your action at Corwen and the many complaints we have received suggest that my view is seriously in error. You will report to your shedmaster when you sign off duty today."

"Er - yessir," replied Lance.

Chester Western Region shed had a new shedmaster after old Sid Thomson had retired, and the new man was not popular.

Lance knocked on the shedmaster's door and waited until he heard a sharp "Come in!" The shedmaster was reading from a pile of correspondence but looked up as Lance walked in. Lance was not invited to sit down and stood in front of the shedmaster's desk feeling like naughty schoolboy up before the headmaster. Shedmaster Barry Tomlinson said nothing for a few moments and then pointed to the heap of papers.

"These telephone notes, Driver Hargreaves, contain complaints from station staff at Corwen as well as passengers on the train you have just brought in." He stared at Lance. "I am sure you know the reason for these complaints. What do you have to say?"

Lance hesitated and then took a deep breath and replied, "I let my prejudice govern my action, sir."

Even if I get the sack, he thought, *at least George would approve of my language - he tried hard enough to get me to improve.*

"Explain."

"We had a Manor, sir, and I recalled that Manors were not really an improvement on the old 43s they were to replace, and I hadn't driven one for many years and assumed they were still disappointing engines. But this one was an excellent engine."

"That was why you jerked the train into action at Corwen?"

"Yessir."

"What about starting at Llangollen and Ruabon?"

"I had no trouble at those places, nor at Wrexham, sir."

"No, you didn't, I checked." The shedmaster took out another sheet of paper from a drawer and glanced at it, "I've also looked at your record and it's impressive, although I haven't forgotten the incident with that lump of coal on the Central Wales line. You haven't been driving long and you were impetuous again; and you have made a bad mistake in not considering passenger safety. However, I always allow my drivers one mistake, *if* there are no very serious consequences. You've now made yours. You understand what I'm saying?'

Barry Tomlinson leaned back in his chair and raised an eyebrow at Lance.

"Yes I do, sir."

"One more bad mistake and you'll be off driving and cleaning the enginemen's bog. However," Tomlinson continued, "Because of what George Denton once told me about you, I'm putting nothing on your record sheet; but I've got a bloody good memory. Now clear out!"

Lance cleared out.

Hmm, Lance mused, *the man might not be a charmer, but at least he's fair. I did make a pillock of myself in Corwen!*

Two weeks later, Lance and Fireman Cardew were waiting at Oswestry to pick up a fitted freight to Warrington routed via Chester and Frodsham. The Welsh crew climbed down from the Manor class engine and Lance smiled as he recognised the driver. He turned to his fireman, "Geoff, meet Driver Dai Gruffyd, an old mate of mine. Poor bugger's based in Aberystwyth in wild wet Wales! How are you Dai?"

"Good to see you again, Lance; but look, this 'yere engine's a Manor!"

"I can see that; so?"

"And it's worried I am."

"Worried? Why?"

"Well I've yeard that you like to shake the stuffin' out of Manors before you drive 'em away!"

Lance glared at his fireman.

"Geoff, what have you been telling people? I thought you were a mate!"

"Nothing to do with your fireman, Lance. It was the Corwen stationmaster. He told me you shook half the passengers out of your train when you took off with your Manor." Dai chuckled, "Along the Welsh coast you're known as the Hargreaves the Hammer!"

"Yeah, well," Lance shook his head in guilt, "Nobody's perfect. Anyway, I was surprised at the Manor, I was expecting it to be a dud."

"Indeed not," Dai's face lit up in pleasure, "They're coming out of Swindon refitted. They're damn good engines now."

Dai Gruffyd's opinion was confirmed by the condition and performance of the Manor as Lance and Geoff took it onto the main line at Gobowen. It ran well and handled the fitted freight with ease. Lance and Fireman Cardew handed the train over at Chester yard to the crew of the London Midland Stanier Mogul 2-6-0 which was to take it on to Warrington. They took their Manor to Chester Western Region shed for servicing and handed it over with regret to another crew who were to take it back to Barmouth on a semi-fast. Their regret was to continue. They had time for a swift mug of tea before their next duty, which was to take a stopper to Salop. Their engine was already serviced and waiting for them outside the shed. Geoff took one look at it when they came out to collect it and muttered, "Looks like it's escaped from Far Tottering or Oyster Creek!"

"What the hell are you talking about?" Lance's forehead creased in puzzlement.

"My missus and I took the lad to London in the summer holiday, to the Festival of Britain exhibition. They had this funny little railway in Battersea Park based on Roland Emett's cartoon drawings. It's called the Far Tottering and Oyster Creek Railway. This here engine could have been designed for it."

"I think I can see what you mean," said Lance as he also caught sight of their engine; it was an old Bulldog 4-4-0 with outside frames. "This old lady is almost 50 years old, and even then was built as a stop-gap, but make no mistake, they've been very handy little engines. There aren't many left, and this'll be due for scrapping soon."

Geoff Cardew gazed at the short roof to the cab and then at the clouds which threatened rain.

"Handy or not," he murmured, "Looks like we're going to have a wet run."

By the time they'd reached Wrexham, Geoff's pessimism was justified; the rain came blasting in from the north-west, rendering totally pointless any attempt to keep dry. Even with the tarpaulin over the cab, the low tender and short roof meant that the two men were soaked to the skin when they reached Baschurch. Nevertheless, admitted Geoff to himself, ancient engine or not, Lance certainly knew how to get the best of the tools he was given. The old Bulldog was still capable of a fair turn of speed on the final run towards Shrewsbury. However, Lance's face began to show anxiety as they neared Whittington.

"What's the matter?" Geoff wanted to know as Lance slowed the train down.

"Not sure," replied Lance, gently lowering the regulator, "But I'm not happy about the engine's riding."

Because of the slower speed, they were 11 minutes late into

Shrewsbury. Once in Coleham shed, Lance stopped the engine and applied the brake. He climbed down to examine the motion but couldn't see anything amiss. He climbed back into the cab, released the brake, and gently lifted the regulator. The engine moved off slowly but then as they ran over a bad rail joint, there was a loud *clunk* and Lance quickly applied the brake once more. He climbed down to see what the problem was and discovered that three of the spring leaves above the front left hand axle box had broken.

"Jesus, Lance!" Geoff's face went pale, "If that had happened at speed we could have come off the road! How the hell did you know something was wrong?"

Lance shook his head, frowning.

"No idea, Geoff. But I fired to George Denton for over a dozen years, and sometimes, it seems, his instincts get into my head."

7 - Lance's narrow squeak (October 1952)

The stopping train to Shrewsbury was a straightforward duty but since the Grange class 4-6-0 was needed for freight work at Wolverhampton, Lance and his regular fireman, Geoff Cardew, took their engine forward for an easy, light engine run from Shrewsbury. Lance drew the Grange into Wolverhampton's Oxley shed, stopped in the main arrival siding and applied the vacuum brake. His fireman turned the tender handbrake on; they didn't know whether the Grange was to be fully serviced or whether it just needed turning and coaling.

Lance had never met the shed foreman at Oxley, which catered mainly for goods work. He and his long-time driver George Denton had always been far more familiar with Stafford Road, the passenger shed, where the Chester to Paddington expresses often changed engines.

Wolverhampton had been an important centre under the GWR because of its huge repair works which had been originally established as the Works for the old Shrewsbury & Birmingham Railway and were still the second biggest in the Western Region.

Lance climbed down from the cab saying, "OK Geoff, I'll report us in to the shedmaster, you pop into the cabin and wet your whistle; I'll join you in a jiffy."

The jiffy, however, was not to be. The shedmaster, sitting in his seat as Lance walked in, stared at the young driver and said, "You'll be Driver Hargreaves, I take it."

Lance nodded.

"I've heard some things about you," continued the shedmaster, "They say you might be young for a driver, but you know the ropes; that true?"

"Not really for me to say," replied Lance, suspecting that a dirty job was about to be sprung on him.

The shedmaster smiled, "I have this on good authority from a bloke who claims to know you quite well; George Denton."

"I've fired to George a few times." Lance was still suspicious and reluctant to give much away.

"I have a little problem you might be able to help me with."

I knew it, thought Lance, *one dirty job coming up.*

But Lance was wrong; the job was more a vote of confidence in his ability as a relatively new driver.

"I need a driver to take a fast, fitted freight to London," the shedmaster explained. "I've got one already but, er…" he hesitated, unsure of himself, "How shall I put this? I am not convinced that the allotted driver has the – um - right attitude today for this particular job."

"Right attitude?" Lance was astounded. *What the hell does the man mean? What kind of attitude do you need to do your regular job?*

"Look," the shedmaster was clearly embarrassed, "I believe the man is unwell but won't admit it. Frankly, I don't want him in charge of an engine today, although I've no problem with his fireman. I understand you know the road too."

"I've only been driving for two years, and I learned the road as a fireman some years back," said Lance.

"Don't worry about that; Fireman McLean knows the road well. I was talking to your boss in Chester. He thinks you could handle the run without any problems. If you take it, it'll take you over the shift time by some margin which will, of course, give you a tidy bonus, and you'll come back on the cushions."

"And my fireman?"

"We'll sort something out for him, shouldn't be a problem."

"Fine, I'll take the freight; what engine have you got for it?"

"It's a 47, and it's already been serviced and coaled; it's ready to pick up the train. I'll take you to it."

Reaching the big 47xx 2-8-0 fast freight engine, the shedmaster clambered up into the cab and addressed the driver.

"Change of duty, Driver Henderson," he said, "Easy work for you today."

The driver looked annoyed.

"Why?' he asked. "We was lookin' forward to a trip to London."

"Something's come up; I needed to change the schedule."

"Yeah, but why us?"

"Not both of you, just you. Fireman McLean can fire to Driver Hargreaves here. I want you in my office in ten minutes."

With that, the shedmaster climbed down from the cab, leaving Lance to deal with a distinctly frosty reception from Driver Henderson. Lance reached out to shake the other driver by the hand in greeting, but his attempt to be friendly was met with a fierce glare.

"What d'you bloody want? You want to drive the fast freight?" Driver Henderson demanded, "Ye're on'y a nipper, still in yer nappy!"

"You're lucky we're on duty," said Lance grimly, leaning forward and seizing the bigger man by the lapels. "If we weren't, I'd kick your arse right off this engine, young'un or not, so sod off!"

In such close proximity to Driver Henderson's face, Lance realised why the shedmaster didn't want him on an engine; there was more than a suggestion of alcohol on the man's breath.

"You're also lucky not to be sacked - you're drunk!"

Lance was angry; drunkenness on duty for a driver was a serious menace for any passengers, not to mention the fireman and guard. It usually earned instant dismissal. Henderson had by this time realised that Lance was not a man to be tangled with and took himself off the cab, muttering inaudible threats.

Lance took a deep breath and introduced himself to the fireman, Hamish McLean. Hamish was relieved that he did not have to fire to Driver Henderson and, shaking his head, confirmed Lance's suspicion.

"You're right," he said, adding, "He's often pissed but he seems to know how to hide it on duty, and I reckon Hendy's dangerous in the cab, but since we've had a couple of union problems in the shed the foreman doesn't want to make the situation worse. The local union rep isn't an easy bloke to deal with."

Lance nodded, "We've had the occasional union versus management punch-up too. I'm in the ASLEF myself, but any union must realise that it's not an employment service. Unions need to recognise there are useless buggers out there who do need to be kicked out, and in our business a poor cabin crew can be a major risk to the public."

"You wouldn't think we had responsible jobs from the pay we get though, would you?" grinned the fireman.

"No, you're right about that. Now," continued Lance, "Let's get on with our responsible job and collect that freight."

He glanced quickly at the fire and was about to make a comment before he remembered that looking after the fire was no longer his job. He was learning, having heeded Jackie Tonks' words about it no longer being his role.

The engine appeared to be in acceptable condition. Seven years after the end of the war and four years into British Railways, the maintenance of rolling stock was returning to a more satisfactory level. Their express freight locomotive was steaming well; these big engines had always been liked by the enginemen, although there were only nine in the whole class. They had been the last class designed by Churchward in 1919 and were strong performers, although the great man had never been overly concerned with the comfort of his engine crews, and the cabs did not offer much protection in inclement weather.

Lance's thoughts drifted back to the cabs of the huge American freight engines on loan to Britain during the latter part of the war years; they'd had well-appointed roomy cabs with comfortable seats instead of the little wooden tip-up shelves the Western engines were equipped with.

Still, he mused, *at least with GWR designs, you know where everything is, whether it's a big King or a little Pannier tank.*

It was late afternoon when they arrived in London, having disposed of their train; Hamish had gone on to the railwaymen's hostel, but Lance wanted to sample the bright lights so he caught a local to Paddington. There he took a tube to Leicester Square and decided to visit one of the new news theatres after a pint at a nearby pub. The barmaid who served him instantly appealed: she was a beauty with an exotic attraction, long black hair and an alluring smile. Her eyes were very dark brown, almost black, and almond-shaped.

Lance tried to chat her up but she was kept busy serving drinks and in spare moments was monopolised by a dark-haired, good-looking young man, so Driver Hargreaves reluctantly decided to finish his pint and head off to one of the news theatres.

After watching the news and a couple of short films for an hour and a half, he couldn't get the bargirl out of his head. He went back to the pub to try his luck again.

She was still there but there were fewer customers and the young man was nowhere to be seen, so Lance was able to talk to her at some length. He was impressed by her views on a variety of topics; she was particularly interested in the new young Queen Elizabeth on the throne. The girl's name was Sally, she came off duty at ten, and agreed go with Lance to a little place she knew of where they could have another drink or two. Lance was delighted; he wasn't on duty the following day, although he planned to catch an early train back to Chester the next morning.

It was well past eleven when they left and Sally asked Lance which hotel he was staying at. Lance stared at her.

"God, I completely forgot to book one," he said and added, "Sorry; that sounds like the oldest excuse in the business, but I really did forget."

Sally laughed, "It's no problem, you'd better stay at my flat, there's a spare bedroom there."

They took the Underground to her flat in Wimbledon. Lance was a little apprehensive; the last time he had accompanied a girl to her flat had been ten years ago in Liverpool and Rosie had wanted money for her services.

Sally however, though obviously rather taken with him, was clearly no tart; she showed him the spare bed and made them a Camp coffee while they chatted for a further hour or so before they went to their separate bedrooms.

However, a little while later, just as he was drifting off into a contented sleep, Lance felt the covers on his bed lift as Sally slipped in next to him.

At six the next morning, Lance woke and checked his watch. *Hmm, almost time to be going*, he thought, but the sight of the naked sleeping girl with her left leg over his was beyond his ability to resist. He hesitated then gently nudged her shoulder.

At a quarter to seven, an unshaven Lance was hurrying over the footbridge south of Wimbledon station when he heard the roar of a train at speed. He paused and looked towards the station, watching a big Merchant Navy Pacific thundering south with a long train. He had heard of these unusual locomotives with their slab-sided shape, and wondered what they were like to drive.

Then, recalling that he was late, he ran on to the station to catch a District Line train from which to change onto a Circle Line train to Euston. Now that the four railway companies had all been incorporated into British Railways, enginemen travelling on the cushions could take the most convenient route, and the ex-LMS route from London to Chester, even with a change at Crewe, was quicker than the old GWR route.

Rather later than he intended, Lance raced up the steps from the Underground and onto his platform at Euston just in time to see the rear lights of the 8am Liverpool express leaving as the train, heavy enough to be double-headed, worked its way out of the platform and up Camden Bank.

"Bugger it!" Lance swore, sighed, turned, and retreated down the steps. He caught the Tube back to Paddington to take the 10.10, which only went as far as Shrewsbury. From there he would have to see whether he could collect a local passenger or cadge a lift in the guard's van of a freight to Chester.

He had an hour and a half to wait so he went to the cafeteria near the open space at Paddington, curiously named the 'Lawn', for a cup of tea and a bun. After that he wandered over to the glass case with its magnificent model of a King class locomotive and its coach made by the Swindon apprentices. He spent a few moments admiring the workmanship before sitting with a newspaper and pondering how he could fiddle another trip to London. He thought of George Denton's usual comments about his philandering, but oddly, this time he imagined the smile on George's face seeming to say, *this one's worth it, and it's time you settled down, my lad!* Lance took the piece of paper from his pocket and looked at the Wimbledon address again; he was determined to meet up with Sally again and had made this clear to her. She had expressed a similar wish but Lance wasn't sure how or when he could manage it. Thinking of a variety of methods to accomplish this kept him busy until his train was drawn into the station by one of the powerful little 1500 class 0-6-0T tanks. They were odd-looking engines with their outside motion and lack of a footplate, but Lance had heard that they were ideal for moving rakes of coaches to and from the carriage sidings at Paddington, and observed this one with deep interest, speaking briefly with the crew before finding a seat in a compartment. There was, fortunately, a quick connecting train in Shrewsbury and he was back in Chester by the late afternoon.

"Lance! Thank God you're back safely!" George Denton's face showed immense relief as he caught sight of his friend reporting in at Chester shed.

"What the hell are you on about, George?" Lance was startled at the reaction to his arrival in the crewmen's cabin. "I know I'm a bit later than intended, but I got involved with a girl you said was worth it."

"You haven't heard? The 8am Liverpool from Euston crashed at Harrow and Wealdstone with more than 400 casualties!"

"*What?*" Lance was horrified. "The 8am Liverpool? And I got into Euston just in time to see the rear lights of it heading out!"

"There were over 100 killed and 300 injured and - wait a moment…" George's hearing caught up with his brain, "What do you mean, I said she was worth it? What girl?"

"I met this bird in London, and you said…" Lance paused, frowning, "Of course you didn't say that, you couldn't have. Why would I think that?"

George gave him a brief, curious look, but the discussion of the terrible accident on the London Midland Region overtook all other conversation that day. It even put all thoughts of Sally out of Lance's head, for a while at least.

One of the older drivers in the shed was loud in his complaints: "The GWR had the Automatic Train Control system working fine in 1912. It would have prevented this disaster. Hasn't it occurred to those idiots at 222 Marylebone Road why the Great Western had far fewer major accidents than the other big three companies?"

There was general agreement among the crews, even among those who had never worked for the GWR. Everyone knew that the GWR had always been different; it had received a good deal of derision for what many saw as its reluctance to introduce more modern locomotives. The last batch of Castles had been built only two years earlier, to a 1924 design. (One engineer at Swindon had shrugged his shoulders and asked why they would need to do anything differently, when their engines were built to very high tolerances and served their purpose with satisfaction anyway.) Nevertheless, the Great Western's superior safety record was acknowledged even by its critics.

After four years, nationalisation with its bureaucracy based in Saint Pancras (privately referred to by railway regional managements as 'the Kremlin'), it seemed, was not providing the solution to the railway problems that many had expected it to.

8 - A final joint effort (January 1953)

Barry Tomlinson, Chester's Western Region shedmaster, was reading a report in his office when there was knock on his door. "Come in," he called. The door opened to reveal Driver Lance Hargreaves.

"Morning, Driver Hargreaves, what can I do for you?"

Despite his previous warning words to Lance, the shedmaster was well aware that Driver Hargreaves showed great promise. He had also decided that he could come to a *modus vivendi* with the young driver, in spite of the latter's occasional truculence. Today however, the young man was, well, almost *subservient*, thought the shedmaster; most unusual. He waited.

"Erm," Lance was clearly ill at ease, "Um - I have a request, sir."

First time he's called me 'sir' with some respect, thought the shedmaster, *must want something quite badly.* He waited again.

"I can't grant your request," he began and noted the rising anger in Lance's eyes. "Until I hear it."

"Oh, er - yessir." Lance was confused for a moment, "It concerns Driver Denton, sir."

Barry Tomlinson found he was enjoying Lance's awkwardness; it didn't often happen.

He frowned, "I don't think we have a Driver Denton on the books."

"Of course sir, I mean *ex*-Driver Denton. He retired in October."

"He did."

"He taught me all I know about driving, sir."

"I can well believe it; he was an excellent driver, but I still don't know what your request is."

"Two years ago I was promoted to Driver, sir, and since then I haven't had the chance to fire to him again."

"No, you wouldn't, would you; you're a driver yourself now." Barry Tomlinson was puzzled; "But what is your request and what has it to do with a retired driver?"

"I want to fire with him just once more for old times' sake, sir."

"And how do you propose to do that?"

"I was hoping, sir, that you could – er…"

The shedmaster's eyebrows shot up. "Are you seriously suggesting I call a retired man back to the job for a day and give him a fully qualified driver to fire for him?"

"Er - yes sir, I suppose I am."

Barry paused for a moment. "Did George put you up to this?"

"No sir, he doesn't know anything about it. It's entirely my idea, sir."

There was lengthy pause, while the shedmaster gazed at Lance, thinking.

"You realise I could finish up before the Divisional Superintendent if it got out that I had allowed something like this?"

Lance's hopes began to rise; it sounded like the shedmaster was giving the matter serious thought.

"Is George still in good shape medically?"

"Certainly, sir; he walks three miles twice a week to keep fit."

Barry Tomlinson thought for a moment, then shook his head. "No, I could not possibly permit such a breach of the regulations. Mind you," he added before Lance could raise any counter argument, "As you are well aware, if a train has passengers, it is forbidden for both engine crew to be out of the cab at the same time. Now suppose Fireman Cardew were coupling up and you were checking

to see if the smokebox dart was tight; imagine that some passenger, dressed as engine crew, were to be seen in the cab; any platform inspector would assume everything to be in order. Then imagine if that passenger were to quietly slip off at, say Wrexham or Ruabon, then I wouldn't know anything about it, would I?"
Lance grinned, "You wouldn't know anything about *what*, sir?"
"A very sound attitude, Driver Hargreaves; now bugger off."
"Yessir."

It was like old times; George had his hand on the regulator of the Saint class 4-6-0 while Lance manipulated the shovel. They were on a semi-fast to Wolverhampton, doing what they had done many hundreds of times over the last dozen or so years. Fireman Cardew was enjoying a ride sitting down for a change, on the fireman's seat on the lefthand side, ready to take over the shovel in case officialdom noticed and wanted explanations. He was also watching two highly competent enginemen working as a very smooth team. Lance hadn't handled the shovel for three years and found that he had missed the vigorous swinging and sheer physical exertion of firing. He was enjoying himself.
"It's a great shame that these old Saints are now being withdrawn," commented George as they were leaving Wrexham.
"Well yes, George," replied Lance, "But they are almost 50 years old and getting a bit rough. Personally I like the Counties; they can match the Saints even though they have their idiosyncrasies."
"*Idiosyncrasies*, Lance?" chuckled George, "My my, your language is really getting quite impressive."
He turned to Geoff Cardew, "You should have heard Lance's language when he first joined the GWR before the war, Geoff!"

"All right, all right!" said Lance indignantly, "So I got a tutor; what's wrong with that?"

"Nothing wrong with that, Lance, it was very laudable," commented George with a smile.

"I bet the tutor was an attractive young lady," said Geoff mischievously.

George began to laugh.

"You obviously know your driver, young Geoff," he chuckled.

The conversation in the cab continued in this vein for some time until George lowered the regulator for the approach to Ruabon. Geoff, still sitting on the fireman's wooden seat, sat up and stared closely at the people on the platform.

"Hey up, I think there's a platform inspector waiting."

Lance leaned out to check then quickly handed his shovel to Geoff, "Quick, get firing, Geoff; it's Mr Dukinfield. He knows George and me and he's a stickler for doing things by the book. George, you'd better get ready to drop down on to the track!"

George instantly grabbed his bag and swung himself out of the cab, climbing down the offside steps until he was standing on the lowest one. He waited until Lance had brought the train almost to a standstill, then dropped off on to the track. He crossed the track, walked up the ramp onto the opposite down platform and hurried into the toilet, from which he emerged a few moments later dressed in his civilian clothes. He waved briefly at Lance and Geoff and sat down with other passengers who were waiting for a down train.

In the meantime, Henry Dukinfield had mounted into the cab.

"Morning, Driver Hargreaves."

"Morning sir," said Lance, "Cold day."

"Yes, and who is this?" the inspector turned to Geoff.

"Fireman Cardew, sir," replied Geoff.

"Have you both been on since Chester?" the inspector asked.

"Yes sir," replied both men simultaneously.

"Mmm," muttered the inspector, "A signalman at Wrexham told me he thought he saw three men in the cab."

"Can't imagine why he would think that," said Lance, frowning.

"You didn't give Fireman – er - Cardew a turn on the regulator, Driver Hargreaves?"

"Oh no sir, Fireman Cardew has only been a fireman for a couple of months, he's nowhere near ready to handle the regulator."

Mr Dukinfield glanced suspiciously at the tender as if to check that there was nobody hiding among the lumps of coal. "Hmmph," he muttered, then nodded to both men and climbed out of the cab.

The two young men looked at each other as the whistle sounded. Lance released the brake and took hold of the regulator. As the train slowly gathered speed, Lance shook his head.

"That was a close call," he said, "The means of getting George into the cab for our last run together again was actually Barry Tomlinson's idea. He's a good bloke for a boss, but I hate to think what he'd do to me if I were to drop him in it."

On their return from Salop, the two crewmen were astonished when another engineman climbed into the cab at Baschurch.

"Just thought I'd have a final check on your driving, Lance," said George Denton. "A goods guard I know gave me a lift me here from Ruabon."

"You'd better keep your head down at Ruabon again then, George," replied Lance, grinning, 'Dukinfield'll be watching us very carefully there. I'm sure he knew something was going on but couldn't put his finger on it."

They took great care as they approached Ruabon, but there was no sign of Inspector Dukinfield on the platform. Lance stared along the up platform and Geoff watched the down platform carefully.

"Must have given up," muttered Lance, staring out of the side of the cab as George eased the engine to a stop. George was crouching low so as not to be visible from the platforms.

"I doubt that," answered George, and he turned to the official crewmen; "Henry Dukinfield doesn't give up easily and he's smart; both of you keep your eyes peeled."

However, it seemed that George was worrying in vain; the only person taking any kind of interest in the cab was a porter. He asked them to take a small packet to a mate of his who would meet them and pick it up in Chester; his friend was a ganger who would be waiting by the buffers of number three bay platform.

Lance nodded absent-mindedly, "Yep, let's have it and we'll pass it on."

He took the packet and placed it near the toolbox on the tender of their 43 class 2-6-0.

The run home towards Chester was straightforward with no incidents, and George and Lance thoroughly enjoyed their final partnership. Lance relished the opportunity to fire to a master driver again – George clearly had not lost any of his old skill - and Geoff Cardew observed how an experienced and well-matched team managed to make the job look so easy and effective. It was a valuable and informative lesson in how to get the most out of a steam locomotive. Both driver and fireman appeared to know each other's thoughts and reacted without any apparent signals. The verbal banter between the two men, who obviously enjoyed a strong friendship, was also highly diverting. Geoff was disappointed when they crossed over the river Dee and passed through the two tunnels; the masterclass was coming to an end.

As they were about to round the right-hand curve into the General Station however, they were brought to a stop at the signal gantry. George grabbed his bag and shook Geoff's hand.

"Nice to meet you, Geoff, but I think I'll drop off here. Lance, we'll catch up in a day or two when you next come to sample Alice's coffee."

Lance looked at George and tapped the backhead, "You're not going to bring her in for one last time?"

George shook his head, "No Lance, I'll hop off here."

With that he swung down from the cab, dropped on to the track, and walked off.

"Surprised he didn't want to complete the job," commented Lance to Geoff, "He's normally fussy about dotting his 'I's and crossing his 'T's."

Their signal rose and Lance lifted the regulator, taking the train into the platform and pulling gently up just before the buffers, where they could see a man in uniform waiting for them.

The man swung himself up into the cab almost before they had stopped and they stared in surprise; it was Henry Dukinfield. He stared around the cab.

"Where's that extra man you had with you in Ruabon?" he demanded, "The porter thought he saw three men in your cab."

"Three men, sir?" Lance was puzzled, "What three men? Why would we need three men? We're both fully qualified."

"The Ruabon porter was fairly sure he saw a third man in your cab."

"I'm afraid he must have been mistaken, sir. Oh, wait a moment - yes; in fact there was a third man; a porter climbed up to give us a packet for a mate here. That must have been who he saw."

"Hmmph!"

Again Inspector Dukinfield left the cab without a word. He was convinced there had been a breach of regulations but he couldn't prove anything.

Reporting to Mr Tomlinson later, Lance explained how they nearly got caught and how they had been lucky to get away with it.

"Lucky?" glared Barry Tomlinson, "Luck had nothing to do with it! I heard that Inspector Dukinfield had been seen on the platform in Chester and I had to send an engine across your track to stop you at the signal gantry where George got off. The only luck was that George took advantage of the stop to get out of your cab."

"Oh," said Lance, grateful to the shedmaster for intervening, though well aware it was not an altogether altruistic act.

The shedmaster had not finished, however, "Now. There's another matter I want to discuss with you. You are getting to be an excellent driver, but you have been in Chester for many years now. In your own interest you may want to consider moving to another shed to gain more experience. I would recommend a double red area like Wolverhampton, Old Oak Common, or Newton Abbot, where you could one day get your hands on the Kings."

Western Region engines had little coloured discs on their cabsides to indicate which routes they were permitted or; red was for the important main lines, and blue, yellow or uncoloured routes were for increasingly lighter lines. The Kings were only allowed on the two heavy routes marked double red from Paddington to Plymouth and Paddington to Wolverhampton.

Lance was startled; he had often thought about doing just that. "Well thank you, sir."

"I'll give you a good recommendation, of course. But," Barry Tomlinson continued, grimacing, "I'll regret losing such an interesting driver; which other of my enginemen throws coal at Spitfires or shakes passengers out of their train in Llangollen?" Lance smiled and shook his head in disbelief; he didn't know what to say.

9 - Domestic developments (July 1954)

Lance had been driving for four years; five if his driving duties during his time as a Passed Fireman were included. He had already gained a reputation for unusual competence as a driver. Many felt he would one day match those skills of his mentor George Denton who, even two years after his formal retirement, was still spoken of with respect.

Consequently, Lance's promotion up the links was rapid and he was already being given express passenger duties which took him as far afield as Hereford and, on occasions, Oxford, Bristol, Cardiff, and North and Central Wales.

His favourite run remained the Wolverhampton, where he would spend time chatting to the crewmen who had what Lance considered the plum jobs of manning the King class engines on the Paddington run. Once on a 'learning the road' run some years earlier during the last war, he had fired a King from Paddington to Warwick and had discovered that, though a glamour job, it was not by any means an easy one. The Kings were only used on the heavier expresses on the northern main line between Paddington and Wolverhampton and they demanded a full input from their firemen. The firebox was huge and greedy, and woe betide any fireman who was not up to the job, or was unfortunate enough to find Yorkshire Hards or Midland coal in his tender instead of the good Welsh steam coal the engine was designed for; the locomotive would show strong resentment at being fed with anything else.

Fireman Geoff Cardew was gazing out of the cab of the big Castle class 4-6-0 on an up express at Shrewsbury and waiting for the connection from the south-west while his driver was on the platform with an oilcan, checking the left-hand slide bar where he fancied he heard a creaking noise.

"Our connecting train seems to be on time, Lance," Geoff called down to Lance, as he saw an approaching train from the Hereford direction.

Lance climbed back into the cab.

"Nothing wrong, as far as I can see," he commented and glanced at the west to north express as it pulled into its main down platform. The London Midland rebuilt Royal Scot class 4-6-0 was already waiting at the north end of the station to take the train on to Crewe and stations beyond, once the Western engine had come off.

"Hey, look at that!" called Geoff in astonishment as the Western engine passed them, slowing down.

"What?" asked Lance, busy with the train journal he was filling the details in.

Geoff was staring in disbelief. "A King's brought the Manchester in!"

"Don't be daft, Geoff," said Lance, looking up. "This is Salop; Kings aren't allowed this far nor...?"

His sentence tailed off as he caught sight of the engine of the incoming Manchester train. "Bloody hell, you're right; it *is* a King!"

Lance and Geoff watched as the huge engine came to a standstill at the far end of the platform and the fireman climbed down to uncouple it. The King moved away from its train and backed down through the station towards the shed at Coleham.

"It's *King George V* as well, *and* it's got a self-weighing tender,"

Lance pointed out as it passed them, "But I don't recognise the crew."

The King had obviously been cleaned and appeared to be in excellent condition as it glided past with only a wisp of steam escaping from the chimney. Lance stared with ill-disguised envy at the locomotive.

"What the hell is a King doing here?" Lance muttered half to himself, "Kings are double red and the route from Bristol to Salop is only single red. They must have changed it without me noticing."

Later that day in Chester shed, he tackled the shedmaster, who expressed ignorance of the matter, but suggested that the authorities were experimenting to see whether the Kings' routes could be extended. Yet when Lance expressed the hope that they might be allowed in Chester, Barry Tomlinson shook his head.

"There'd be too many weight and loading gauge restrictions Lance, between here and Salop," he stated, "They wouldn't fit in the bays at Chester, we'd have to use Platform Fourteen all the time and the London Midland wouldn't like that."

That evening at home, Lance's mother said to him, "I need to have a serious talk with you, Lancelot."

Lance knew this tone; something was up but he couldn't think what it was.

"You are 34, my son, and still haven't settled down. Since your father died five years ago, I have kept house for you, but I too am getting old and I need a rest. I want to move into a home for the elderly."

This was a shock to Lance who had assumed, without thinking about it, that his mother would be there for him for as long as he needed her. He was by no means unfeeling; it just hadn't occurred to him that he would be a burden to her. He nodded, instantly contrite.

"I'm sorry, Mum," he replied, "I must admit that I have taken you for granted."

He was ashamed of himself, "How do you want me to help you?"

"I shall sell the house," his mother said, "And there will be sufficient money after the sale to allow you to get a small flat somewhere, and…" she paused for a moment, "I want you to move away from Chester."

Lance couldn't believe his ears; surely he hadn't been such a dreadful son?

Before he react, she continued, "Your dependence on me is holding you in Chester where you can't drive those Kings you talk about so much. I want you to move to where you can drive them; Wolverhampton or Birmingham, is it?"

Lance smiled at her. He'd had no idea he talked about those engines quite so much!

The next few months were emotionally charged for Lance. On the one hand he felt he was abandoning his mother and feelings of guilt were plaguing him and on the other hand he had applied for and obtained a position at Wolverhampton's Stafford Road shed, where half a dozen Kings were shedded.

The Stafford Road shedmaster, who knew why Lance had applied to move there, warned him that although he had been driving express passenger trains, he could not expect to get on to the Kings straightaway. He would have to learn some of the roads around Birmingham, for which the Wolverhampton Division was responsible.

Lance was happy with that. He knew that he was moving in the right direction.

He hadn't been in his new flat in Wolverhampton more than a week or two when a letter arrived for Lance. It was from Sally and Lance did a double take as he noticed the postmark; Chester. What on Earth was she doing in Chester? As it chanced, he was on an Oxley to Crewe fitted goods the next day and he arranged to come back from Chester on a slow goods.
He caught a train from Crewe to Chester in time to allow a quick visit to the address in Hoole that Sally had given him, near the General Station. He and Sally hadn't any formal - or come to that even informal - agreement. They simply enjoyed each other's company and met whenever they could manage it, which wasn't too often bearing in mind their respective addresses. Nevertheless, since he had met her, he had been far less interested in meeting other girls (although there had been one or two who had been willing to accommodate his libidinous inclinations).

Sally met him at the door with a kiss and led him into a small flat. He sat down in the lounge and Sally fetched him a beer while she made herself a cup of coffee. She had an expression on her face which Lance hadn't seen before, and he wondered what it could signify. She didn't appear to be angry or disappointed, although she knew he had moved away from Chester. If he was reading her right, Lance thought it was more an expression of apprehension.
"Look Sally, I had no idea you were going to move from London," he began, but she interrupted him, holding up her hand and smiling.
"That's not why I wanted to talk to you, Lance," she said, "I got

offered a very good job, which pays far better than barwork, and accepted it. That it was in Chester was a bonus – for me at least. I know you have transferred to Wolverhampton, but we can still see each other from time to time."

"Yes," said Lance, "And we will be able to see each other probably more often because I'm regularly on the Chester run."

"There's something else you should know," she said hesitantly.

"What?"

"Last time you were in Wimbledon, I told you we were – er - *safe*," she said.

"Safe?"

"Yes, you know – in bed."

Lance froze; "We weren't..?"

"No."

"Um - are you..?" He didn't seem to be able to finish his sentences.

"Yes. Two months."

"Oh my god, Sally!" he gasped, then, "We shall have to get married!"

"No," she interrupted firmly, "I am not going to force you into a marriage. The fault was mine, and you are not going to have to pay for it. My new job will pay well; I can manage."

"You don't mean to find a doctor who..?"

"Certainly not, I want this child, and abortion is illegal anyway."

"But I've just transferred to Wolverhampton and can't get a transfer back!"

"You don't need to. I said, I can manage. My parents will help as well. They're going to move up here too."

Lance stared helplessly at her. "But I..."

"Lance," she said firmly, "I am 29, and I've worked in bars for years. I've made plenty of tips; but bar work is not for me any more. My sister's got three kids and I love them and want one of my own. Now I'm getting one, and I'm happy about it. If we got married, we wouldn't stay married for too long. You love your big engines and would resent me if I took you away from them. No, we're not getting married, and that's flat."

Lance knew Sally well enough to know that further discussion on the topic would be pointless.

In the Stafford Road shed the following week Lance was called in to the shedmaster's office.

"How many times have you taken a Castle on the Chester run, Driver Hargreaves?" the shedmaster asked.

"A Castle to Chester?" Lance asked, "I really couldn't say, sir; I've done it so often with either a Castle or a County and twelve on."

"So you are familiar with heavy passenger trains northwards; have you learned the Paddington run?"

"Not well sir; I learned the road once in 1942 during the last war. I haven't been on it much since."

"I see. Well I want you to learn the road to Paddington thoroughly; I need another two or three drivers in that link. We've had a few retirements recently."

It was always useful for drivers to learn as many routes as possible. It extended their route knowledge and was a factor when promotion was being considered.

"Ever taken an express passenger to Brum or Oxford?"

"Yes sir, the night sleeper to Oxford a few times; why?"

"I need a driver to take the 2.15 as far as Snow Hill."

Lance frowned, "20 minutes? I don't see any difficulty there, sir."

"You'll come off at Snow Hill and Driver Fletcher will take it on to Paddington."

As it turned out, the short run to Snow Hill was quite straightforward.

"How'd you go, Lance?" Driver Albert Fletcher grinned at him as he climbed into the cab at Snow Hill.

"Easy as pie, Bert; it was a doddle. To be honest, a 28 with a long heavy unfitted goods is harder to drive than a Castle on an express, in my book."

"I'd be inclined to agree with you, but I'd never tell an Oxley man that!"

They both laughed; they knew that either of them could find themselves on a goods engine from time to time. Starting a long goods train was tricky; the wagons had to be pulled into motion carefully one by one if you didn't want to break a coupling. It could take a few minutes before all the vehicles were in motion, and taking a heavy unfitted freight downhill was even more tricky as the weight of the train could mean loss of control.

A few days later, Lance was visiting George Denton.

"So Lance, how do you like driving down south?" George tapped his pipe out and placed it on the mantelpiece of his lounge fire before putting on his slippers to go with Lance into the dining room where Alice was laying the table for lunch.

"No problem so far, George," Lance said with some enthusiasm.

George nodded, "No, I didn't expect you to have any difficulties."

"How's that young lady of yours, Lance?" Alice broke in, "George tells me she's moved to Chester. We'll have to invite her round."

"I'm sure she'd like that, Alice," replied Lance, "She hasn't made many friends here yet."

"It really is a great shame that you transferred to Wolverhampton just as she moved to Chester," said Alice.

"It is," agreed Lance, "If I'd have known she was coming here, I wouldn't have asked for a transfer."

It was a fortnight later when Lance brought Sally over to the Dentons' for a cup of coffee in the afternoon, to meet George and Alice. They clearly approved of the young lady, and later as Lance went to the hall with George to fetch the coats, George pulled him aside and whispered to him.

"Good job you brought her now Lance, before Alice notices Sally's condition. Alice can be funny about things like that and I'll need to prepare her."

As George was drying the dishes in the kitchen later, Alice came in.

"What a nice young lady Lance has met, George. Such a pity that he lives so far away; she's going to need help with that baby on the way."

10 - The new apprentice (October 1955)

Young Mick Sinclair was depressed; he looked around the Wrexham's Western Region locomotive shed at Croes Newydd with distaste. The place was dirty and littered with piles of ash and coal dust around the tracks leading to the shed itself. His shoes were already filthy.

Mick had arrived with polished shoes less than half an hour before – "in order to make a good impression," his mother had said pointedly.

It was a fair point, he thought; he badly needed to make a good impression after he had been sacked from the three jobs he had already tried.

"Ye're no use ter me, boyo," his last boss had said, "Ye're lazy, irresponsible and ye don't listen to instructions."

Mick was annoyed; all he had done was to leave the chuck key in the lathe when he turned it on. The huge key had been hurled off the lathe at high speed but it hadn't hurt anyone; why make such a fuss about a little mistake anybody could make?

He watched as an express passenger passed the junction, slowing down to stop at the station. The big engine hauling it was impressive though, and Mick could see himself in a year or two – certainly before he was 20 - sitting in the cab of one of those mighty Castle class engines speeding south to Paddington. He had always liked fiddling with machines but even at school in the technical classes his teachers had frequently berated him for his inattention to their silly rules. He would soon show them; they could stick their stupid regulations once he was a top link driver (he didn't know quite what that meant, but he had read somewhere that these were the senior drivers) doing a ton with main line expresses. He would learn quickly what the best dodges were for getting ahead. In the meantime he had to try and keep his nose clean in the new job his mother had organised for him.

Freddie Rowntree ('Sweetie' to the other lads in the cleaning gang, although not within his hearing) shouted to him, "Come on yer lazy bugger, get cleanin'!"

Mick sighed, looked at the lump of cotton waste he had been given, and joined the cleaning gang.

"You can do the left hand side of the smokebox," said Freddie, who was the gang leader, "And then clean the top, but watch your step; it's a long way down."

During the half hour lunch break, Mick asked Freddie how long it took to become a driver.

"It varies," replied the gang leader, "In the Western you are a Cleaner doing increasingly responsible jobs until you're ready to take the exams for fireman. Then you're a Passed Cleaner an' can fire to a senior driver who can keep an eye on you. You are ready for promotion to Fireman when a vacancy occurs, but you might 'ave to change sheds. When you've got plenty of firin' practice you take your driving exams and become a Passed Fireman an' again a Driver when there's a vacancy somewhere."

The mention of exams was a worry; Mick had been a reluctant student at school and had left as soon as it was legal to do so.

"Yeah, but how many months does all that take?"

Freddie hooted with laughter. "*Months?* It takes years, lad," he said, "This is quite an important shed with more than 50 drivers, and I don't know of any of 'em under 30!"

Mick was horrified. "But what about the top link; driving to Paddington an' that?" he said plaintively.

"Here," said Freddie, "The top link will 'ave you driving to Phwlleli or Birkenhead. We don't supply drivers for the Paddington run; to do that you'd need to transfer to one of the really big sheds like Chester, Salop or Wolverhampton."

This all sounded very disappointing to Mick. "What if I ask for a transfer to Chester?"

"Wouldn't make too much difference," replied Freddie, "You'd still 'ave to go through all the cleanin' jobs first."

"What are the more responsible jobs the cleaners have to do?"

"Well," began Freddie, thinking, "There's fire lighting, cleanin' ash pans and firin' the stationary boiler, for instance."

"The stationary boiler?"

"The old boiler on brick pillars for dryin' sand an' other jobs."

"And I've got to do all these before I can drive?"

"Yes, but once you've shown some responsibility, you might get asked to ease an engine a few yards – say over the ash pit or under the coalin' stage."

"When can I do that?"

"Whenever a driver wants you to, but he'd have to trust you to do it properly first."

All this didn't sound too promising; it might take months or even years, unless..? Mick wondered whether he couldn't persuade one of the drivers to let him drive an engine. Once he had his hands on one, he was sure they would realise his potential and promotion would rapidly follow. He decided to check out the drivers to see if he could befriend one of them and wangle a bit of driving on the quiet.

In point of fact, it was 18 months before Mick got his hands on the controls of a locomotive. He had been doing most of the simpler jobs in the shed, which all cleaners had to work their way through before anyone felt they were safe in the cab of an engine. Apart from cleaning engines, he had shovelled coal from coal trucks into the coal hoist, carried some of the fitters' tools and watched them make apparently impossible jobs look easy; he had fired the stationary boiler and had even lit the fire in a cab once or twice. In short, he had become a familiar figure among the many enginemen in Wrexham Western Region shed. His only disappointment remained that it was primarily a local shed, albeit an important one, and did not contain any big passenger locomotives apart from a Manor or two; although it was a moot point whether these light 4-6-0s could be classified as 'big'.

One morning he was called into the shedmaster's office. He worried about this as he had been fairly certain nobody had seen him steal the two small shifters a careless fitter had forgotten to put into his bag. Mick thought he could get a bob or two for them in the local pub. The shedmaster and the foreman cleaner were both in the office.

"Cleaner Sinclair," began the shedmaster, "I want you to go to Bala this morning for a week's work there. They are a man short in their cleaning gang, and I think we can spare you for a few days. You will travel in the cab on the afternoon train; it'll be good experience for you. Accommodation has been arranged for you in the town. You can take the morning off and collect whatever you need for a week away."

"Thank you, sir." Mick was pleased at this apparent recognition of his service. He left the office and hurried home to boast to his mother of a potential promotion, as he saw it.

"I think you should also warn the shedmaster at Bala to watch the lad carefully, Ned," said the foreman cleaner to the shedmaster after Mick had left the office, "I'm certain the young bugger's light fingered, although I have to say, I've never actually caught him at it."

"I've sometimes wondered about that too, Fred; he's a smart Alec and a cocky little sod. I'll be glad when he's off the shed for a while; I just don't trust him."

Mick was disappointed at the work in Bala shed; it was exactly the same sort of work he had been doing at Croes Newydd, but the shed was far smaller and he was under closer supervision. He had to curb his inclination to petty larceny while he was there; a senior man always seemed to be in the offing and he had no opportunity to slip a tool unobtrusively into his overall pockets.

He was involved in emptying the ash pan of a Pannier tank one morning and during his morning tea break he asked a passing engineman why there was a red notice at either end of a little 0-4-2T. The notice read 'Not to be moved'.

"That means there's probably a bloke checking the inside motion. It's a tight fit in there and those big cranks are huge and heavy, four or five tons in a big engine; if they move even an inch when he's squashed up against one of them he could be badly injured."

Inside motion? Cranks? thought Mick, *Who's interested in all that inside stuff? I want to know how the cab controls work.*

He nodded, attempting to show some interest. He was still on the look-out for a driver who might let him drive an engine a few yards.

"How hard is it to drive an engine?" he asked the driver.

The latter considered for a while.

"The actual driving's not that difficult once you know what you're doing. It's the rules you need to remember; they govern the safety of the train and you have to know them very well indeed. It also depends on where you're working; on a relatively quiet run such as the Trawsfynycd branch it's not too bad, but on the main line out of Salop or Chester you need to have your wits about you." He glanced at Mick as if measuring him up, "How long have you been a cleaner?"

"About 18 months," replied Mick.

"If you get stuck into your rule book, it might not be too long before you can qualify as a Passed Cleaner; then you might be given some firing jobs, and young firemen are occasionally given the regulator by their drivers - under strict supervision, of course."

"Do cleaners ever get to drive?" asked Mick innocently.

"That's rare," said the driver, shaking his head, "And even then only when the driver can trust the cleaner for a couple of yards or so. Too much risk involved, and up before the shed foreman if anything goes wrong!"

The week at Bala ended and Mick went back gratefully to Croes Newydd where he felt he could supplement his pay with the odd spot of thieving.

One evening an unusual event occurred; a Castle from a Chester express had been failed and was on the turntable siding being seen to. It had 'Not to be moved' notices fore and aft and there was a fitter's bag on the ground next to the engine. Further back in the siding behind the turntable there was a heavy Collett 0-6-2T tank engine waiting to move forward for turning. Its driver, Frank Jackson, was talking to Driver Ianto Hughes and he turned and called out to his fireman, "Bring her forward onto the table, Andy!" Mick could see that Fireman Andy Pugh was talking to another driver behind their engine and obviously couldn't hear what his driver was calling.

Mick seized his chance and climbed swiftly into the cab where he released the handbrake of the tank engine and lifted the regulator gently. The engine began to move. The feeling of power as this heavy locomotive began to move under his direction gave Mick an almost unbearable thrill; but it was almost across the turntable before he lowered the regulator, and it continued to coast on, slowing down gently. It was only 15 yards from the stationary Castle before Mick realised and applied the brake. The engine slowed and only then did Mick hear the frantic shouting from Driver Jackson by the lineside.

"What's he on about?" muttered Mick guiltily as he quickly slipped down out of the cab on the side away from the shouting drivers. The locomotive gave the Castle a gentle nudge before it stopped. From behind a nearby wagon he saw Drivers Jackson and Hughes and a couple of other enginemen hurrying to the Castle, which had been pushed about a foot backwards. Mick darted behind a heap of ash and scurried away before anyone could see him. He joined a gang cleaning a pannier tank, his heart beating wildly.

"Who the holy hell moved that Collett?" roared Driver Jackson in a fury, "Who had the bloody controls?"

He caught sight of his fireman Andy Pugh hurrying towards the now stationary tank engine.

"Andy!" he yelled, "Who did you get to move our Collett?"

"Nobody, Frank," Andy shouted back, "I didn't know you wanted it moved."

"I called out for you to move it onto the turntable."

"I didn't hear that!"

"Well somebody drove it!"

In the meantime, Ianto Hughes and several other nearby men were lifting out a fitter who had been inside the Castle. He was bleeding profusely and left a trail of blood as they carried him into the enginemen's cabin. The insistent clanging of an ambulance bell could soon be heard.

Fifteen minutes later, Cleaner Sinclair was called into the shedmaster's office. The shedmaster looked at him grimly. "Were you in the cab of that Collett?"

"No sir."

"Where's your cap?"

"Dunno sir, I must have dropped it somewhere."

"Is this it?" The shedmaster produced Mick's cap and placed it on the table.

Mick Sinclair picked it up and saw his name in it. "Yes sir, that's mine."

"It was in the cab of the Collett."

"Someone must have put it there, sir."

"You were seen running from the cab."

Mick Sinclair realised he had no way out of this. He shrugged his shoulders and said nothing. *Bugger!* he thought to himself, *I'll lose a fair few bob for this. God! I could even get the sack!* He worried about what his mother would say.

"Fitter Jeffries was in that Castle working on the inside motion."

"He might have got a bit of a jerk then."

The shedmaster's face registered disbelief at the remark. "*What did you say?*" he snarled.

Mick Sinclair felt that he might have been too flippant; and tried to amend his attitude.

"I'm sorry; I admit it, sir. I'll pay whatever the fine is for touching the controls without permission."

"Pay a fine? *Pay a fine?*" the shedmaster was beside himself. "When that engine moved, the crank swung round and crushed Fitter Jeffries' chest. The man's dead, you stupid little idiot. You'll be bloody lucky to get ten years!"

11 - 'A snatch in time' (November 1956)

Lance was feeling his way forwards in the cold, thick fog south of Shrewsbury; he and fireman Harry Paisley were taking a heavy unfitted goods from Manchester to Cardiff. They had taken over the locomotive from a Chester crew at Shrewsbury and were to hand over to a Cardiff crew at Hereford. They were well behind time, as was every other train on the Welsh border. The fog was playing havoc with the timetables.
Their train was signalled into a long siding while a North to West express rumbled slowly past them, its fireman gazing earnestly out of the cab side, keeping a sharp eye open for the signals.
Lance pulled out his watch from his waistcoat pocket and looked at it.
"Poor bugger's already 70 minutes late and I bet he doesn't know exactly where he is," he commented.
Harry looked at him and asked, "Do *you* know where we are?"
Lance stared at Harry.
"Of course I do!" he replied indignantly, "We're just north of Leominster. So get your detonators ready in case we have to use any of them."
The fog detonator was a small but loud explosive device with lead straps which could be wrapped round a rail, to warn an oncoming train of a signal at danger; it was set off by the engine's wheel running over it. A few minutes later their signal clanged and they had the clear to move out back to the main line and continue their journey.
Lance appeared hesitant, however, and he kept his hand on the

regulator in a manner which suggested he was going to close it again. Harry looked at him curiously, wondering whether Lance could either see something he himself couldn't, or knew something that Harry was unaware of.

Lance was feeling his way forward, his forehead furrowed as if he were concentrating on something.

"What?" Harry enquired.

"Something's not right," said Lance, leaning out of the cab and gazing along the track.

"What's not right?"

"Don't know," answered Lance slowly, clearly unsure of himself, then shutting off steam rapidly and stopping the train.

"Cow on the line!" he called as the train stopped. They were passing a field and a gated crossing had been left open.

"Quick Harry, nip out and chivvy that cow back into the field before it gets itself run over."

Harry did as he was asked; he was a country boy and knew how to deal with cattle. The cow was soon back in its field and they moved off again.

"How did you know about that cow?"

"I had a sense about something wrong; I get this on rare occasions."

"A useful sense to have," commented Harry, continuing conversationally, "When we were kids my little sister once thought I had a similar sense."

"How come?"

"We had found a wind-up gramophone and some old 78 rpm records in the attic, but the labels on the records had faded badly. I told her I could still tell what the tunes were."

"Of course – you just had to play them through the loudspeaker."

Harry smiled as he remembered, "No; I just held a needle tightly in my fingers and the vibrations told me what they were. Annie thought it was magic!"

The fog was getting thicker as they progressed south, and some time later Lance lowered the regulator once more and slowed the train gently; the slowing down had the effect of buffering up the trucks gradually, but if the driver wasn't careful, their combined weight and inertia could push the train further than the driver intended.

Harry watched Lance's train control with silent admiration as, with a distant, gentle *clunk*, the guard's van at the rear of the train stopped. The fog was getting thicker and visibility was down to no more than four or five yards.

Harry gazed out of the cab.

"We might even miss the signals in this muck," he grumbled.

Lance glanced out of his side of the cab as the train was at a standstill.

"Have a dekko at the signal now, Harry," he instructed.

"The fog's far too thick; how d'you expect me to see a bloody sig..." grumbled Harry, then he stopped and stared in disbelief; the base of a signal post was visible directly next to their cab.

"Distant and home signals both clear!" Harry said formally then swung round and glared at Lance; "How the holy hell did you know where to stop?"

Lance grinned, "I know this run well, I've been down here with George Denton hundreds of times."

"Don't give me that," answered Harry, "That doesn't explain how you came to stop right next to the signal in this pea-souper."

Lance savoured the moment; "Yes, well I've just seen a fence I recognised where the cattle gather under a tree in the corner near the railway. We've been held up at this signal many a time."

As he spoke, he lifted the regulator and the train eased away with the trucks' couplings clanking as they picked up pace. A long unfitted goods needed very careful driving as there were no vacuum brakes to assist the driver to control the train's braking; a snatch could break a coupling and part the train. Such a train on a hilly run was one of the most difficult trains for a driver to handle, and the engine's brake, in connection with the brake on the guard's van, were all that held it. Both the driver and the guard had to know the route well in order not to lose control. It wasn't unknown on a goods train coming downhill for the fireman to drop out and run along the train, dropping the wagons' brakes by hand.

Passenger trains all had continuous vacuum brakes which were under the direct control of the driver. He could apply the brakes to every vehicle simultaneously, which made the train far simpler to handle.

However, even knowing the status of the section in front of them, Lance and Harry felt their way cautiously forward in the mist, ready to stop at any moment if necessary. The cold mist and the constant strain of staring ahead into the gloom sapped their energy and both men took a quick and frequent turn standing in front of the fire with the firedoors open. Harry was thankful that at least they had plenty of coal and the engine was steaming well; he had to take care not to allow the locomotive to build up too much steam and blow off.

"I bet you haven't had many worse journeys than this down this run," he said to Lance.

Lance shook his head. "This is nothing; once during the last War, George Denton and I ran a heavy Salop stopper with a Hall; we then had to take the Hall on to Bristol with the empty coaches which were needed at Plymouth."
"So what was so hard about that? A Hall could manage a dozen ECS."
"At Salop we had six more LMS corridors added to our own 12, and no pilot engine. We had to take 18 35-tonners on this hilly run to Bristol with the Hall and no chance to top up the tender!"
"Crikey!"
"When we got to Bristol, the tender was empty and the relief crew at Temple Meads weren't happy! But we were both knackered and just left the train to them and went straight to the hostel."
"How did you manage through the Severn Tunnel?"
"With difficulty. If George hadn't helped with the firing, I'd have been wiped out. As it was, it was all I could do to get to the hostel; I didn't even want to go for a beer or check out the local talent."
"Gee, you must have been dead beat!"

The rest of the run required the same level of concentration, as the fog persisted almost to Hereford. The two footplatemen were relieved to finally see lights emerging from the murk. The fatigue brought about by the need for continuous staring for signals and looking out for other possible dangers was extremely wearing and hardly alleviated by the ease of firing due to their slow progress. Their tea in the enginemen's cabin went down instantly and was followed rapidly by a second mug.
"Put that down as a bugger of a trip, Harry," commented Lance as he contemplated a third mug of hot tea.

"Variety being the spice of life," nodded Harry, "Can't remember who said that."

"Yes, well not all trips are that bad," said Lance, "I've had some wonderful trips with an engine in good nick and co-operative signalmen. There's something about driving a steam locomotive that you don't get with the electrics or the new diesels."

"Yeah," smiled Harry with a grin, "I know what it is; greasy overalls and coal-blackened hands after your shift!"

Lance laughed. "Yes, there is that; but that's not what I mean. The feeling of raw and visible power with a huge mechanical machine, and the fact that you're responsible for 500 tons doing 80 miles an hour is just magic! One run like that makes up for all the lousy runs – and you'll get plenty of them too."

Harry nodded. "I've got to say, in spite of the dirt and hard graft, I do enjoy this job."

Their return to Wolverhampton was far less stressful as they had to take a large Prairie 2-6-2T tank engine light as far as Worcester where they picked up a local passenger back to their home shed. The run in the warm, enclosed cab of the Prairie and the fact that the fog had lifted had raised their spirits somewhat by the time they reached Stafford Road shed.

After several months of working together, the two men found themselves beginning to feel like a team, essential for effective management in the running of a steam train. Under Lance's guidance, good nature and matching wit, the young fireman was learning his trade well. Lance had been to see the shedmaster to ask whether he could have Harry as his regular fireman and the boss had agreed. But there was to come a time when Lance nearly lost his team-mate.

They were running slowly back from Paddington after bringing in a Birkenhead express. The coaches had been drawn back to the carriage sidings for servicing and their Castle class 4-6-0 was standing at a signal, waiting for the route to be cleared. They were heading back to Old Oak Common shed to be turned and coaled before taking the 12.10am sleeper back as far as Wolverhampton. Harry stood at the top of the cab steps and asked nervously, "Anyone about watching us?"

"Why?" asked Lance curiously, "What are you planning to do?"

"I'm bursting for a pee," replied Harry, undoing his fly buttons. He felt his collar grabbed very firmly and was dragged backwards into the cab.

"What the hell..?" he gasped, "There's nobody about!"

"Go and piss on the coal." growled Lance, shoving Harry towards the back of the tender.

"On the coal? That's not nice!"

"Do as I say!" Lance's voice had a bite that Harry had not heard before.

Without a word, the fireman walked to the back of the tender and relieved himself there, then returned, buttoning his trousers.

"Finished?" asked Lance grimly.

Harry nodded.

"Right then; a few questions. Firstly, how long have we been working together?"

"Almost a year now."

"Are we getting to be a team?"

"I thought so."

"Yes," said Lance, "So did I. Next question; where are we exactly?"

Harry glanced out of the cab, "We're waiting near Subway Junction."

"Right, and what lines are we next to?"

"Only the Underground surface tracks."

Lance paused, then asked, "Did you do any science at school?"

Harry scratched his head, "Science? Yeah, why?"

"How about basic anatomy?"

"Some." Harry was getting very confused.

"Okay. Now, what happens when a stream of liquid, say for example piss, lands on a live rail carrying 600 volts?"

Harry frowned and then turned deathly pale.

"And what happens," continued Lance, "To your family jewels when the 600 volts hit them?"

Harry shivered at the thought.

"You're getting to be a good fireman, Harry, but you'd be no use to me back on the 12.10 Birkenhead with fried balls! You'll have to learn that being on a footplate is not just the occasional run in discomfort like the one we had to Hereford recently. George Denton nearly lost a young fireman who caught his shovel on a signal mast once, and a fireman at Newton Abbot was beheaded by a tunnel as he climbed on his tender to shovel the coal forward. If you're not careful, it is very easy to die in this job."

12 - Lance gets technical (August 1957)

Lance had arrived in Chester once more and had a couple of hours to kill while he was waiting for his return run to Wolverhampton. Sally was on holiday with their son, waiting in Lance's flat, and they were due to travel together the next day for a week in a caravan in Newquay. They had decided on a caravan because of the independence it gave them; that and the fact that as they were not married, a hotel might be unwilling to accept them.

Sitting in the enginemen's cabin, Lance was delighted to see his old driver George Denton enter, accompanied by his 14-year-old grandson, also named George.

"How are you, George?" asked Lance, shaking George Senior by the hand then turning to the boy, "And what about you, young feller? I've been hearing good things about your school reports!"

"I'm fine thank you, Uncle Lance," replied young George.

"Look Lance," said George Senior, "Give me a few minutes, I want to have a quick chat with Marty Smith."

Marty was finishing his tea when George approached him, "I'm sorry George, I'm on a shunting duty and just finished my tea break. Our chat'll have to be another time."

"Hang on, Marty," said Lance, "I have an idea; what if I do half an hour's shunting for you, while you yak to George here? I can take young George into the cab with me; it'll be good for him to see how dirty the job can get."

Marty turned to his fireman, "What d'you think, Joe?"

Marty's fireman nodded, 'No skin off my nose, Marty; I'm all for it!"

"Come on, young George," said Lance and they left the cabin.

Some time later in the cab of the big Hall class 4-6-0, the youngster asked Lance why they were shunting with such a big engine, observing that Halls were normally only used for long distance trains.
"Smart kid," commented Joe, pausing in his firing.
"You're quite right, George," said Lance, "But we're using the Hall to make up its own train. We often do that, if there's not too much collecting to do. This engine is taking a South Wales goods train up to Hereford where a Cardiff engine will take over."
"Engines are very complicated, aren't they Uncle Lance?" said George, gazing at the many dials and levers in the huge cab.
Lance paused as they waited for a shunter to walk over and couple up a line of vans. "Actually, George, they're not. A steam locomotive in its essence is a very simple machine; it's the machinery to control it that makes it seem complicated." He turned to the fireman, "Joe, take over the driving for a bit while I explain to George how a steam loco works."
Joe nodded, happy to get the chance to do a bit of driving.
"Now George," said Lance, "Imagine a huge can filled with water."
George nodded.
"Now put a hot fire underneath it. What happens?"
"The water boils and forms steam."
"Right, and what happens to that steam?"
George thought for a moment, then said, "Not sure."
"It expands," said Lance, "And has to escape before it blows up the huge can. Now, imagine that big can is the locomotive boiler… So that the steam can escape, the engineers added two small

cylinders, one either side, with a moving disc of matching size on a rod - the piston - so it can move back and forth. Alongside each cylinder is an even smaller valve cylinder with connecting holes - called ports - at each end, and a piston shaped like a long cotton reel. Live steam from the boiler is fed into the ends of the valve cylinder, while an exhaust pipe from the middle leads to the chimney. Now, when the valve is forward, live steam flows to the back of the piston in the big cylinder and drives it forward. At the same time, the valve moves backwards and the front port remains uncovered under the middle of the cotton reel, allowing any steam already in the cylinder to escape past the middle and up the chimney as they move. Are you with me so far?"

"I think so," said George slowly, "When the big cylinder fills with steam and reaches the back end, the valve gets to its front end, and it all happens over again - I mean live steam enters the front port to drive the piston back and the rear port is uncovered to allow the first gulp of steam to exhaust past the cotton reel. Then it happens again."

"Exactly," smiled Lance.

"As I said; smart kid," interposed Joe, grinning.

"That wall is called a cylinder head, and it's connected to a rod on the outside of the cylinder..."

"A connecting rod?" guessed George.

"Right again!" said Lance with approval, "This rod turns a wheel which is coupled to other wheels and together these wheels move the engine. Simple!"

"I always wondered what the difference was between connecting rods and coupling rods. But," continued the boy, staring at the cab's backhead, "What about all these dials and levers?"

Lance shook his head, "Just refinements, George. The basic principles were developed by James Watt and George Stephenson more than a hundred years ago, and they haven't changed; they have only been improved on."

"So the engines with all the refinements are now super efficient?" Lance smiled again, "What percentage of the energy from the coal do you think the steam locomotive converts to useful power?"

Joe looked over from his driver's position, "Yes, Lance, I've often wondered about that too."

"Have a guess, George."

George shrugged his shoulders, "Um – 80?"

Lance sent a questioning look at Joe, who added, "I'd say a bit less than that, Lance; about 70?"

"A really efficient steam locomotive," replied Lance, "Can expect to extract between ten and 12 per cent of the energy from its fuel."

"*Ten* per cent?" both Joe and young George were astonished.

"Your granddad, young George," continued Lance, "Was told so by a Swindon engineer. He also told him that the big American diesels were only a few per cent more efficient. Electric locomotives are far better at about 60 per cent, until you take into account that their electricity comes from coal power which reduces their overall efficiency to only somewhat better than the diesels."

George was quiet for a few moments, then he said, "In my *Eagle* there's a picture of a planned atomic railway engine."

"Your eagle?"

"It's a kid's comic, Lance," explained Joe.

"Yes," added George with enthusiasm, "It's got Dan Dare in it; he's a spaceship pilot and he fights the Treens from Venus."

By this time the goods train had been fully marshalled and Lance took over the driver's position to bring the train into the departure siding. Then, after screwing the tender brake on hard, he left the cab with George and they walked across the tracks back to the enginemen's cabin where Marty Smith was chatting with George Senior.

"Thanks for that, Lance," said Marty, "I owe you one."

Marty said goodbye to George and went out to join his fireman.

"Did you really know that a steam locomotive is only ten per cent efficient, Grandad?" asked young George.

George Denton looked at his previous fireman. "What have you been teaching him, Lance? Have you been pontificating?"

"He's a bright lad, George; it's a pleasure to talk to him. Look, I have to get back on shift soon, but I'll be in Chester again next week. What say I'll pop over and have a cup of tea with you and Alice?"

"We'll look forward to it."

George Senior nodded to his grandson and they headed for the door.

"Oh, young George,' called Lance, "Give my regards to Dan Dare and his Treens!"

Lance's next duty took him to London and, while waiting for his engine to be turned and serviced, he listened in the enginemen's cabin at Ranelagh Bridge to the discussion, which was getting heated. The Old Oak Common men were generally agreed that the Western Region Castles were superior to the British Railway standard Britannias, whereas some of the Cardiff Canton men were equally adamant that the Britannias were fine engines and equal to the Castles any day. Unfortunately for the ex-GWR men, the statistics appeared to support the views of the Canton drivers; the Britannias were clearly able to perform on a par with the Castles, at least on the South Wales runs.

Jeremy Finnegan of Old Oak Common turned to Lance and asked him what he thought; "You're a Wolverhampton man, Lance, and neutral. What d'you reckon to the Brits?"

Lance was silent for a moment then observed, "I haven't a lot of experience with the Brits, but I've heard that the Cardiff Brits are always kept in good nick." There were murmurs of agreement from the Canton men, but he continued, "If you compare them to the newer Castles, I doubt there'd be much in it."

The Old Oak contingent expressed some disappointment to hear this, but Lance added, "On a Plymouth run, I'd pick a Castle first, but only because I am more familiar with them and I know they can do the job."

"What about Paddington to Chester?" one of them asked, "You know that run well enough."

"That's a two-engine job," replied Lance, "I'd want a Castle, or preferably a King to Hampton…"

"… and a Castle to Chester," another driver added.

Lance shook his head, "A Castle if it's not a heavy train."

There were disbelieving looks from both sides of the argument. "Not a Castle?"

"I'd want a County, especially a redrafted one," Lance said, "Best of the lot for a heavy train on a hilly run. The same applies from Salop to Hereford, you can't beat 'em on those routes."

"Good for you, Lance!" this came from a Plymouth driver, "To Penzance or Newquay, a County with a dozen on, you're laughing."

These views were regarded by many drivers as sacrilege.

"But their tractive effort is less than that of a Castle," claimed one driver.

"Tractive effort?" ridiculed Lance, "Don't make me laugh; are you trying to tell me a Hall is more powerful than a Star was because it's got a higher TE?"

There was amusement among the drivers; the last Stars had only recently been withdrawn but they had been generally popular with the drivers for their strength and speed. They had been the pinnacle of express passenger locomotives, on a par with the French engines (which Churchward, their designer, had studied very carefully) before 1920.

The GWR Halls had been a very successful general purpose locomotive which Stanier had used as a basis for his own brilliant Black Fives, designed when he transferred from the Great Western to the LMS.

Collett, the successor to Churchward as the GWR Chief Mechanical Engineer, had sacrificed some of the Star's ideal proportions due to loading gauge limits in his later Castles and Kings, in order to obtain greater power and haulage ability.

On his return to duty four days later, Lance was called in to the shedmaster's office. This was always something of a worry and Lance cast his mind back to consider how he might have raised the ire of Mr Harrison.

"You been with us for three years now, Driver Hargreaves?"

"Yes sir."

"And you've been driving for what - seven years?"

"Yes sir." Lance couldn't imagine where this was going, but there was no indication that anything was amiss.

"I've been on the phone to Barry Tomlinson about you," continued the shedmaster. "The fact is that I'm in a quandary. I need another regular driver for the top link duties and your name has been out forward. You are a trifle young still, but Mr Tomlinson maintains you're good for it. What is your own view?"

Lance scratched his head to try and gain some time to think; he was staggered by the suggestion, but there was no doubt that he would agree.

"I'd like to try it, sir," he replied.

Mr Harrison nodded, "Right, well you can start as of now. I'll give you a week on trial. As it happens I need a driver for the Paddington this morning. Your fireman is Fireman Paisley."

Lance was pleased he could continue working with his regular fireman. Like Lance himself, Harry was young but competent in his job. It seemed to be a good start to the day.

It transpired that the day was proving to be even better when Lance found the board with the train details on it; the engine designated for the Paddington was 6006 *King George I*. He was going to drive his first King! Lance had fired them several times to Paddington with different drivers and had, of course, frequently driven Castles; but the mighty Kings were the prestige engines of the Western Region. They were undergoing redrafting and were proving to be masters of the heaviest expresses between London and Wolverhampton on the main Northern route and between London and Plymouth in the West Country. There was talk of trying them out on the South Wales run and extending their range to Shrewsbury for the Cambrian Coast Express.

At Wolverhampton Low Level station, Lance backed his King onto the five coaches, which were to strengthen the ten coaches on the train from Birkenhead, which had arrived behind a Castle with a Chester crew. He waited while the Castle uncoupled and moved off to the shed for servicing before backing his own coaches onto the train and waited for the departure time. When the guard waved the green flag, Lance gently raised the regulator and was thrilled by the way the great locomotive eased its long and heavy train out of the station without the slightest hesitation. He couldn't believe the sheer power in the King; he had often driven the very similar Castles but the King was something else. It had 6' 6" diameter wheels instead of the 6' 8" wheels of the Castles; but while this gave the Castles an extra turn of speed, there was no doubt that the Kings had the edge on sheer power.

By the time they had reached Paddington, Lance was both physically drained yet elated; he had reached just over 80mph twice and was sure that with experience he could better this. As he sat on the wooden tip-up seat, waiting for Harry to uncouple the engine so that the coaches could be drawn back to the carriage sidings, he felt a deep satisfaction with his job. He was perfectly well aware that there would be times in the future when he would swear at and curse these engines, but equally he knew that driving these magnificent locomotives was what he was made for.

13 – Lance meets a Duchess and gets political (March 1958)

The old 43 class 2-6-0 mixed traffic engine had clearly seen many better days. Lance and Harry were pulling up with a Salop to Snow Hill stopper at Codsall but the engine was reluctant to pull the eight lightly loaded coaches – a job for which it ought to have been easy. It was wheezing from cylinders and joints and hadn't seen the inside of the paint shop for so long that the letters 'G W R' could still be discerned on the faded paintwork on the side of the tender.
"I suspect this old girl will be heading for the scrap line at the Works soon," commented Harry to Lance.
Lance nodded, "Yes, and she's not the only one. I've seen some of the plans for the railway modernisation; no steam on the Western by 1965; they'll all be gone."
"No steam?" Harry was astounded, "Then why are they still building 9Fs at Swindon? Doesn't make sense!"
"Two reasons, Harry," said Lance, "We still need reliable locomotives until the diesels are working properly."
"And the second reason?" prompted Harry.
Lance grimaced, "The second reason, Harry, is that MPs are elected according to their popularity not their bloody intelligence! That the railways are moving ultimately to diesel power is fine; it makes sense. What doesn't make sense is to rush the whole business before they are tried and tested."
"How else would the railways manage?"
"Easy; there are plenty of steamers in all regions that just need to be modified to give them years of extra life. Look at our Counties;

with the redrafting they're fine engines, same as the Kings and Castles."

"But the 9Fs are fine engines," objected Harry, "And building them gave work to a lot of men who needed work."

"Of course," agreed Lance, "But it would have been cheaper to use the men to maintain or even rebuild some of the various heavy freight engines of the regions until the diesels were ready. Let's face it; all four of the old companies designed engines entirely suited to their duties. Swindon, Doncaster, Crewe and Eastleigh could have managed and there would have been no need for the expense of designing, tooling and building brand new engines which are now going to be scrapped years before they are due for it." Lance was getting into his stride, "Look, by 1939 the big four companies had all developed the types of engine they needed; they had the skills and expertise required. Then the war came and the government took them over; by 1945 the railways were run down to buggery and the government in its wisdom did little to help them before taking them over and letting the bureaucrats loose on them to tell railwaymen how to run a railway."

Towards the end of this tirade, they heard a call from just outside their cab.

"Oi, you fellows, what's your beef with the 9Fs?"

They both turned to look at the adjacent down line where they saw the grinning face of a driver in the cab of a 9F; he had a string of wagons filled with scrap metal.

"Nothing's wrong with them – they're damn good engines," replied Lance. He glanced at the wagons, "But you could have managed this lot with an 8F and there would've been no need to build all these BR engines. All the companies had developed satisfactory engines; they just needed proper maintenance after the war – and they never got it!"

The 9F driver nodded, "Aye, well you're probably right there." Just then the down signal cleared and the 9F driver said, "Hey up, we're off. Pity, I'd like to have chatted a bit more; where're you based?"

"Stafford Road, why?"

"Ever get to London?"

"Yes, we're often on Paddington expresses."

"How'd you fancy a run on a Euston express? I could squeeze you in the cab, although I couldn't take your mate as well."

The 9F slowly moved off as the driver yelled back, "Get to Camden shed next week and ask for Driver Ted Harvey!"

"Hmm, might take him up on that," commented Lance as their own signal dropped and they began to move off, their locomotive wheezing. "That's if we ever get anywhere with this engine."

Camden shed was familiar to Lance, as he had occasionally (and illegally) had a cab ride back from Euston to Wolverhampton High Level in a Midland Royal Scot 4-6-0 express passenger engine. Camden was the London Midland Region's large passenger shed and supplied the enginemen for the expresses from Euston to the north. Lance met Ted Harvey and told him that he was to travel from London back home on the cushions in three days' time. This coincided with a trip north that Ted was running and they agreed that Lance could get a cab ride as far as Stafford and catch a local back from there.

On the appointed day, Lance found himself in Camden shed locomen's cabin supping a mug of tea with Ted. He had arrived earlier than agreed and had used the time to look around the shed

and once more to admire Stanier's magnificent Duchess class 4-6-2 Pacifics which had been designed to handle the heavy Scottish expresses. Their huge, long lines spoke sheer power. Originally, in 1937, many of them had been streamlined, but the streamlining had been gradually removed as it hampered maintenance and was not effective in regular traffic speeds. Lance expressed his admiration of these engines to Ted who nodded in approval.
"You'll get a better idea of what they can do today, Lance," he said, "You'll be in one as far as Stafford!"

"I'll have to concentrate a bit, Lance, until we're well out; the climb out of Euston takes a lot of attention."
The Duchess had 16 coaches on and the load would require all of the engine's 40,000lbs of tractive effort to get the train up the hill. Nevertheless, the big engine powered up the grade with little sign of serious effort.
"Bet one of your little Castles couldn't do this so easily," smiled Ted as he took the heavy train past the carriage sidings and Camden locomotive shed.
"Possibly not," admitted Lance, then smiled, "But in 1910, one of our Stars showed the LNWR how to get out of Euston without gasping and without a pilot!"
"Yes," admitted Ted, "I read about that. But then in 1933 the LMS got its own back on the Great Western; we pinched your best man, William Stanier!"
"That's true," replied Lance, "We missed out there; and later, our man Hawksworth didn't get a chance to show much as the war stopped him."
"It didn't stop Bulleid from building his express passenger engines

for the Southern; those Merchant Navy Pacifics!"

"No, that's true; but then he pulled the wool over the eyes of the wartime authorities; he classified them as mixed traffic engines and had them photographed pulling freight trains, the crafty bugger!"

By this time they were accelerating through Watford Junction and heading for Tring cutting in the Chilterns. In spite of himself, Lance was deeply impressed by the power of the big Pacific, and the ease with which it hauled its heavy train at speed.

"Any actual disadvantages in these huge engines?" asked Lance.

"Not for me," responded Ted, "They'll do pretty much anything I want them to do, but the firemen aren't always so impressed. They need a lot of coal between Euston and Carlisle and this makes big demands on the fireman; they have a steam-driven coal pusher in the tender to assist, but the bloody thing can be temperamental."

Ted's fireman, Jack Winslow, nodded vigorous agreement as he put his shovel down for a moment to mop his brow. "Ted's right there, you're easily knackered after you reach Lancaster and have to get over Tebay."

Lance had been watching Jack for a while and then offered to take over the shovel to give him a breather.

"You can watch that I don't make a dog's dinner of your fire!" he said.

He thought he could see what was required. He found to his surprise that he actually enjoyed firing again; he hadn't fired for several years apart from spelling his own firemen occasionally.

Jack watched carefully, smiling, "You haven't lost your touch, there'd be a job for you in Camden if ever you want one!"

"No thanks," said Lance, "I still prefer to drive big engines!"

"Big engines?" queried Ted mischievously, "I didn't think the Western had any big engines!"

"Size isn't everything, Driver Harvey," said Lance with a grin, "Our Kings might only be 30-year-old 4-6-0s, but they can still match your Pacifics. I can get one out of Paddington on the hilly Birmingham run with 16 on and no pilot, no problem at all!"

The banter between the two drivers went on, much to the amusement of Jack, who took over the firing once more. Lance had crouched down in the cab during their stop at Rugby in case authority in the form of a Platform Inspector was about, and he was equally careful at the next stop in Stafford. Here he thanked Ted Harvey and slipped out of the cab inconspicuously, to join other passengers waiting for a connection to Wellington and Wolverhampton.

The following week, Lance and Harry were scheduled to run a Birkenhead to Margate passenger; they had relieved the Chester crew at Stafford Road and were to take the train, with a Chester-based County class 4-6-0 at its head, on to Oxford where the County would come off and a Southern engine and crew would take the train further. This was a new run for Harry who had not been down this route before except for 'learning the road', observing where the signals were and familiarising himself with the route.

"Very interesting place, Oxford," commented Lance as they were sitting in the enginemen's cabin, "You know, I believe it's unique from a footplateman's point of view."

"Why's that then?"

"Keep your eyes peeled while we're waiting for our return shift, young man; you'll see what I mean."

"What am I supposed to be looking for?"

"Anything that an engineman might be interested in," replied Lance cryptically.

They both watched as their recent train moved out southwards towards Didcot, now with a Southern Region Lord Nelson class 4-6-0 at its head.

"What d'you reckon to those Nelsons?" asked Harry as the train disappeared on its way to the south coast.

"We should be grateful to them," replied Lance, "They gave us the Kings!"

"They what?"

"When the Southern Railway built them in 1926 they had a tractive effort greater than our Castles, which meant that the Southern could claim to have the most powerful express passenger locos in the country. This claim annoyed the GWR's chairman so much that he told Collett, the Chief Mechanical Engineer, to build something bigger. A year later we had the Kings!"

"Funny, the Nelsons always remind me of the early Royal Scots," mused Harry.

"There's a good reason for that too," responded Lance, "In 1926 the old LMS was looking for better engines for their Scottish expresses. They asked the GWR for Castle drawings, and even asked Swindon to build some for them, but apparently the GWR wasn't having any, so the LMS asked the Southern, who gave them the Nelson drawings. They used those to help build their Royal Scots."

After their County had been turned and serviced, Lance and Harry took it back to the station to pick up a return semi-fast passenger to Birmingham. As they waited with their train on the main down platform, they watched a York to Bristol north to west express pull in. The Eastern Region B1 4-6-0 uncoupled and a Western Region Hall coupled up to it. Harry stared at Lance; his face registered sudden smiling realisation. He pointed to the local passenger to Bletchley waiting in the bay platform with a London Midland Region tank engine.

"I know what you were talking about now!" he grinned, "You get engines from al. four regions here!"

"Full marks, Harry!" chuckled Lance, "You're not as daft as you look! I don't think there's any other passenger station in the country where you can see that on a regular basis."

14 – Lance meets his match (July 1959)

The short freight being made up by the crew of an 0-6-0T Pannier tank was an all-stations pick-up goods from Hereford to Gloucester. It would stop at each small station and the bored shunters and porters would get their hands on it and play trains while the engine crew watched, amused, and drank their tea. Some of the small local stations had to deal with only two or three trains a day and the staff relished the chance to do some real railway work. This usually entailed merely attaching or detaching a couple of general merchandise wagons and a coal truck for the local coal merchant. For the crew of the pick-up goods, Driver Jack Henderson and Fireman Sid Jenkins, the run was not arduous and the locals were normally friendly and pleased to see them. The shift made an occasional pleasant break from the more demanding work of a heavy freight or express passenger. There was the added advantage in the possibility of acquiring a freshly killed rabbit or pheasant in exchange for letting a shunter handle the regulator in the sidings (under strict supervision, of course), as long as the signalman could be trusted not to report what he saw.

The two enginemen of the pannier, having made up their train, were back in the crew cabin for a brew-up. They still had half an hour before they were due out.

The shed foreman popped his head into the cabin and said to them, "You two'll be coming back from Gloucester light engine this evening. Just make sure you get that Pannier back to me in good nick; it's needed as the station pilot tomorrow as my regular Mogul's off to the Works at Caerphilly for a sole and heel."

Jack nodded, "Aye we'll do that."

They finished their tea and set off back to their train, climbed into the cab and waited for the signals to let them out on to the main line to Gloucester.

The first two stops at little country stations followed the usual pattern as the shunters made a big deal of marshalling the empty wagons, attaching them using several unnecessary moves. Jack and Sid chuckled indulgently at their antics.

At the next stop, Fawley, they paused at the platform before backing into the small goods yard. Two enginemen stepped out of the station waiting room and approached the cab.

"Can we cadge a lift to Gloucester?" asked Lance Hargreaves, "We're due back in Wolverhampton by tonight after an emergency shift. Your foreman knew we were over our shift, but he said that a bit of extra work wouldn't hurt us."

"Yes, he can be a bit awkward at times, but on the whole he's not too bad."

Jack recalled that an emergency earlier that day had called for a couple of enginemen to run a light engine to Gloucester, but wondered why these two had been left here in Fawley.

"He might be alright to his own men, but for enginemen from another Division like us he needs taking down a peg or two. OK if we climb in?"

"Yes of course," answered Jack, "Hop aboard."

"Ta, we got this far and two Gloucester men took the light engine over. The foreman at Gloucester must have forgotten that they were here."

"Yeah, but why didn't you continue with 'em to Gloucester? You'd've got back to 'hampton quicker."

"True enough," replied Lance, lifting a bag, "But we got a couple of coneys from a mate of the shunter here. He only charged us a bob."

Jack nodded, "I'd check 'em carefully though for shotgun pellets. We know Mervin's mate; he's none too fussy about how he catches 'em. The local butchers won't have a bar of him."

The slow run to Gloucester passed pleasantly; Lance's fireman Freddie Jackson gave Fireman Jenkins a break from firing and Lance, who knew the road, took over some of the driving. They even offered to stable the Pannier in Gloucester shed so that Jack and Sid could catch an early passenger train home to Hereford; but Jack explained that the engine would be needed in Hereford the next day.

"You'll still need it coaled and watered," said Lance, "We can at least do that for you."

"You don't mind?" asked Jack, "That would give us a chance for a cuppa before we return."

"No, you did us a favour; just go and get your tea, we'll take the engine to the shed."

While driving to the shed, Lance said to Freddie, "That shed foreman at Hereford didn't need to give us that light engine duty, we were due to return on the cushions but the bugger often gives extra work to men from foreign sheds. One day I'm going to sort him out."

Whilst at Gloucester there was a reported derailment near Stroud and an engine was required to go and assist.

Lance smiled at Freddie, "This little Pannier would be ideal for the job; it's still got enough coal and water for such a short run. Let's volunteer it!"

"But Lance, the engine is needed in Hereford." Freddie was unhappy at the thought of arousing the ire of a foreign shedmaster.

"Yes it is, isn't it?" Lance's voice held a distinct note of satisfaction. He stopped by the Gloucester shedmaster's office and let him know that a Pannier was available.

"Good man!" said the shedmaster, looking up from his paperwork, "Thanks for that. I was wondering where I could find a spare engine. I suppose you and your mate are not er..?"

"No sir," answered Lance quickly, "We've had an extra long shift and are into overtime anyway and have to get back to Wolverhampton tonight."

"Ah well, just thought I'd ask; I'm not really short of a crew, but the engine was a problem. Look, there's a train to Brum in twenty minutes; you two can catch that and get to Wolverhampton from Snow Hill."

Lance sat on the platform at Gloucester and watched with some satisfaction as the Pannier took a couple of linesmen's vans on the line to Stroud. He had already ducked into the enginemen's cabin and told Jack and Sid that he'd been overruled by the Gloucester shedmaster and hadn't been able to prevent the Pannier from being taken. They both nodded; they knew that it wasn't wise to argue the toss with shedmasters. Lance hadn't wanted them to get the blame for his act of revenge.

The following week saw Lance and Freddie on a Birmingham to South Wales semi-fast passenger. They had picked up their train at Snow Hill and would hand over to Cardiff men at Gloucester. Their engine was a Grange class 4-6-0, universally regarded by Western enginemen as free-running and with a forgiving nature, and it had no trouble handling the 11 corridors, so their run was straightforward and without any undue difficulties.

"If we can get a similar run back to Brum then home, it'll have been a pleasant shift," commented Lance to Freddie as they pulled in to Gloucester where the Cardiff men could be seen waiting on the platform. However, Lance's optimism turned out to be unjustified. In the enginemen's cabin with a welcome brew, the shedmaster stuck his head in and told then they were to be rerouted and would have to take a Mogul 2-6-0 with nine coaches on a slow passenger to Shrewsbury; from here they could go on the cushions back to Wolverhampton.

"But don't worry," he told them, "I've contacted your foreman at Stafford Road and he's agreed."

"Oh shit!" muttered Freddie, "That means we go through Hereford again. I hope the Hereford shedmaster doesn't know about us coming through."

"Why should he?" Lance was unperturbed, "There'd be no reason for him to check on crewmen passing through."

"I suppose you're right," replied Freddie doubtfully, "But I'll be happier when we leave Hereford."

Freddie would shortly discover he was wrong about this.

At Hereford there was a Hall class 4-6-0 standing next to the down platform. "Looks like we're to have an engine change," commented Lance, "A shame really; this Mogul is in good nick."

The driver of the Hall climbed down from his cab and into theirs while his fireman went to uncouple the Mogul from their train.

"Sorry lads," said the Hall driver, "This engine is urgently required on shed, but you can take the Hall on the train to Salop. Since you're Wolverhampton men, the shedmaster says you can take it light engine on to the Works there; it's due for some maintenance."

"But the Gloucester shedmaster said we could go on the cushions from Salop to Wolverhampton," complained Freddie to the driver. "By the way, does he know who we are?"

"I dunno," said the driver, surprised, "I didn't ask 'im; 'e's not the sort of bloke you ask questions of; yer just do as yer told. It's easier that way."

"What's the Hall like then?" asked Lance.

"Again, I dunno, we only brought 'er from the shed, but I know she's bin oiled and coaled enough to get 'er to the Works. She seemed OK."

He nodded to the two men as they climbed down and into the Hall's cab. It was clean enough, which was usually a good sign.

"Mmm," muttered Lance, thinking hard, "I wonder if..."

He didn't pursue the thought out loud. Their signal dropped and they moved forward past their coaches and over the crossing to back down on to the train. Freddie dropped down to the track to couple up and Lance checked the vacuum brake when Freddie called up that the coupling up was complete.

Their starter signal dropped, the guard showed his green flag, and Lance released the brakes, lifting the regulator gently. Nothing happened, so he lifted it a little more and with a tired *choof!* the engine began to move. It instantly became obvious why this engine was to go to the Works; there were squeaks and groans from most of its moving parts, and Freddie found himself shovelling hard far earlier than he had expected. He had great difficulty maintaining sufficient pressure to keep the train moving at much more than a snail's pace. A Hall with only nine non-corridors should have had a very easy duty.

"Good job we're only a slow passenger to Salop," said Freddie in between bouts of heavy shovelling.

"Yeah," muttered Lance thoughtfully; he too, was having a hard job trying to keep time with an engine which clearly didn't want to. He was strongly tempted to fail the engine when they finally reached Leominster 20 minutes late. Arriving late didn't look good on an engineman's record unless there was a compelling reason, but failing an engine led to an inordinate amount of paperwork and could even raise questions regarding a driver's competence. Furthermore, reasoned Lance privately, they were still within the Hereford shedmaster's area of influence, and he didn't feel like facing the man if he didn't have to.

The remainder of the journey to Salop was for both enginemen a nightmare experience and the only minor let-up came with the final run to the Works. The engine was definitely due for serious attention; indeed, Lance mused, in view of the new policy of dieselisation, it was quite likely that the locomotive, one of the early Halls, would be scrapped rather than repaired. Already the scrap lines at various sheds were collecting steam locomotives at an increasing rate. He had even heard that the last of the latest BR 9Fs were being constructed and the whole steam locomotive building programme was due to end in the following year.

It was several months before Lance and his regular fireman Harry Paisley found themselves in Hereford shed on a tea break. This time they were to return via Worcester to Birmingham with a short fitted freight. Lance was feeling slightly nervous and was half expecting a call to the shedmaster's office but was relieved when they were on their engine, an elderly Mogul 2-6-0, and moving out onto the main line to Worcester. The engine was one of the very early batch and was no longer capable of being driven with any kind of panache; indeed, it was steaming badly and the shaking in the cab was a strong indication of other matters needing urgent attention, possibly worn big ends or coupling rod bushes. In fact, by the time they finally reached Birmingham, Lance had to recommend that the engine be failed for further duties until it had been seen to by a fitter.

It was another month before their next run from Hereford, this time with a Bristol semi-fast, matched with another engine in deplorable condition. The climb up through the Severn Tunnel was so slow that they almost feared they would stall before they exited the tunnel. This was particularly worrying as enginemen caught in a smoke-filled tunnel had actually suffocated in the past.
"I was chatting to a bloke in the cabin at Hereford," said Harry as they were walking through the Bath Road shed at Bristol, "He asked if your name was Lance Hargreaves."
"Why did he want to know?" asked Lance curiously.
"He said the Hereford shedmaster wanted to pass on to you his best wishes for another comfortable run. What the hell did he mean? This has been a lousy run."
Lance just shook his head without replying. Putting one over the Hereford shedmaster had definitely not been one of his better ideas.

15 - *Vale!* Driver George Denton (July 1960)

The funeral was a major event and the little church in Upton, a quiet residential part of the outer Chester suburbs, was overflowing. Apart from the 30 or so footplatemen, fitters, storemen and clerks from Chester's Western Region shed, there were senior officers and even the Divisional Superintendent was present.

Driver George Denton had been a popular figure in Chester shed as he had always been prepared to encourage the young cleaners into climbing the ladder from Fireman to Driver as far as they could. He had made a point of giving his own firemen a stint on the regulator to accustom them to driving and to spell them from their onerous firing for hours on end. He had also been widely respected throughout the Division as one of its very best drivers.

Even though it had been eight years since his retirement, George was still regularly talked about and his advice had become legend. One or two of his recommendations had even made it into the enginemen's rulebook.

Lance had taken the train to Chester early that morning, picked up Sally and her son from their house in Hoole, an inner Chester suburb, and taken a taxi to Upton. Young Billy held tightly on to his mother's hand as he looked around at all the strange people, several of whom were talking to his Uncle Lance.

"Who's this then, Lance?" asked Marty Smith, staring at the lad.

"He's Billy, Marty," replied Lance, "Sally's lad."

Marty glanced at the boy and then at Lance with a measuring eye. "Is he now?" he asked with a grin.

"I heard you got a medal for a spot of bravery during the war," said Sally, deftly moving the topic of conversation to a less tricky area. Marty shrugged, "It wasn't a big deal, to be honest, I just acted without thinking; it was more that railway training took over."
"Well I think it was very brave anyway," said Sally, which endeared her to Marty and, more importantly, took his mind away from where it had clearly been going.

More than one person had already remarked on the similarity in appearance between Billy and his 'Uncle Lance', and the topic was one that Sally and Lance tried hard to avoid in public. The five-year-old knew he was missing a father but since Uncle Lance was a frequent visitor to his house (often staying the night), Billy didn't feel the absence of a father as much as one might have expected, and his uncle commonly accompanied him and his mother on excursions. There was occasional comment from neighbours, but this was rare because they had learned to be circumspect where Sally was concerned; she gave any gossip in her hearing very short shrift, and those inclined to it quickly discovered that gossip and innuendo could be two-edged swords. One of her neighbours had remarked, smirking at a party in their street, how fortunate it was that Billy's Uncle Lance looked so much like him. Sally had agreed and added that it was almost as fortunate as the neighbour having such a nice man friend who came to look after her whenever her husband was away on business.

The funeral service was short but dignified and the congregation were generally impressed by the tone and content of the sermon. Reverend Harper, who had known both George and Alice well for many years, had taken the theme of 'Well done thou good and faithful servant', from Matthew's Gospel. Those who had known

George well felt that there could not have been a more suitable quotation, and even the agnostics in the congregation nodded in recognition of the aptness of the topic.

A wake had been organised in the local village hall where tea and scones, as well as beer and sherry, were accompanied by comments to the effect that there were no more drivers like George, and that the coming demise of steam meant the death of real skill among railwaymen.

"Don't you agree, Lance?" asked one retired driver.

Lance shook his head, "No Jack, I can't say that I do. I've already had a few trips in the diesels and I think that while the requirements are different, there are other challenges that good drivers will have to face, and specialised skills will be needed and developed by those with the will to do so."

Lance was by now frequently on the London expresses and found himself quickly at home driving the big Kings; he had long enjoyed driving the Castles, Counties, Halls and Granges, but the Kings were for him the perfect heavy express engines. He had admired the Duchess Pacifics of the London Midland Region and assumed that North Eastern and Southern men regarded their A4s and Merchant Navy engines with similar appreciation, but for him the Kings, which had recently been modified with improved drafting and new double chimneys, were supreme in spite of the fact that they were over 30 years old. With slightly smaller wheels than those of the Castles, they had the edge in sheer power yet could, given the opportunity, manage 90 miles an hour with relative ease.

Their improved performance and strength was particularly welcome at this time as the West Coast main line was being electrified, and the consequent interference in the LMR timetable gave the Western Region main line to Birmingham and Wolverhampton added traffic, which the Kings were well able to cope with. Yet even for these engines, the writing was on the wall; once the Euston to Crewe section had its new electric locomotives there would be little need for the heavy express steam locomotives. Even the big London Midland Pacifics were likely to be relegated to comparatively minor duties.

Lance had decided to enjoy his last few years on the steamers as far as he could. His diesel experiences had, however, convinced him that his future career still lay in the cab; standing all day in a signal cabin or parked on a chair in an office was not for him.

"What the hell are those people doing?" Harry Paisley paused in his shovelling as he gazed out of the cab of the Grange en route from Birmingham to Cardiff as they were slowing down at a home signal showing 'danger'.

Lance brought the train gently to a stop. He glanced over to the large barn in a field where Harry was pointing. Once the train stopped they could hear a roar from the barn; a car pulled up and a man got out holding a cage with a chicken in it.

"The bastards are cockfighting, I bet," said Lance angrily, "But I didn't think they would hold a fight right near a railway line. I can't stand cruelty to animals; as a kid I used to join a group which scattered bits of meat and bones where we knew there'd be a fox hunt; it used to distract the dogs and drive the hunters wild, spoiling their fun."

While he was talking, the signal dropped and Lance reached for the regulator, easing it upwards and taking the train slowly off again. A few minutes later they pulled up at Honeybourne.

"Listen Harry," said Lance, "Killing for fun is a foul business and a police matter. Nip over to the stationmaster's office and tell them to contact the local plods to look out for the cockfight. They might be able to nab the sods."

Harry was back in a jiffy with a grin on his face. "There happened to be a copper in the office as I went in; he was delighted when he heard what we saw. He said they knew there was a fight on somewhere but they couldn't pin it down; now they know where it is, he said they'd have 'em within 15 minutes. He said to say thanks to you!"

Lance nodded in satisfaction, "It's odd the way the public take railways for granted," he remarked, "You know Harry, we were right next to that barn with a whole trainload of people but that cockfighter with his caged cockerel totally ignored us!"

"Yeah, I know what you mean, Lance, I was stuck once at a signal with a slow goods, and my driver and I watched a burglar climb through the window of a house. He looked around first to see if anyone was about but we were only about 20 yards away and he didn't see us at all, the daft bugger!"

"What did you do?"

"Wasn't much we could do aside from report it to the next signal box; the bobby there would've contacted the boys in blue, I suppose."

As they were leaving Newport, Lance remarked to his fireman, "Did you know, Harry, almost 30 years ago this run was a pointer to the future in railway terms."

"How d'you mean?"

"The old Great Western tested one of its new diesel railcars between Brum and South Wales, because passenger traffic was down."

"Those ones they used to call the 'Flying Bananas'?"

"Yes, that's them."

"What happened? I've never seen one on that run."

"No," chuckled Lance, "They proved so popular that traffic increased too much for them and they had to be replaced with a regular train again!"

"So they didn't work out?"

"Of course they did; the GWR built a lot more – and some are still running. The LNER built some and even the LMS built a set, though it never ran much."

"What happened to it?"

"It came out just before the war and ran between Oxford and Bletchley, but was withdrawn when war broke out. After the war they were more interested in their two big diesels and ran them as a pair from Euston to the north."

"So the LMS led the way?"

"No they didn't!" snapped Lance indignantly, "We did; all the green diesel mechanical units running about now are a direct result of the GWR's experiments."

"But the big LMS diesels laid the way for our main line dieselisation programme," said Harry mischievously, "The GWR wasn't responsible for that!"

Lance looked at him and shook his head sadly. "Wrong again, Harry. The change to diesels is based on American and German research. The Yanks have been running diesel trains for years, and the Germans have built a very successful V200 class diesel engine, while we have been getting Mr Riddles to design new steam engines. We can't seem to decide which type of diesel suits us best."

The conversation continued in this vein intermittently, whenever steam was shut off, allowing the two men to converse until they reached the outskirts of Cardiff and had to slow down as they approached Cardiff General station. Here Harry climbed down from the cab to uncouple their Grange, which they ran on to Canton shed where the engine was stabled. In spite of the banter, both men felt that they worked together well as a team and enjoyed each other's company, yet Harry occasionally felt the urge to try and get one up on Lance. His driver was undoubtedly knowledgeable in his railway history, but he could be just a tad smug at times, and Harry often looked for an opportunity to knock him off his perch. So far he hadn't succeeded.

They admired the appearance of the engines in Canton shed; the shedmaster had a reputation for keeping his engines looking spick and span and it showed. The Cardiff men were proud of their locomotives and pointed out to the two Wolverhampton men that they weren't the only ones to run Kings; Cardiff was to be given a few as well.

Back in the enginemen's cabin over a mug of tea, Harry had a sudden thought, "Your wonderful Swindon hasn't got a great record in modern traction though, has it?"

"What d'you mean by that?" Lance's tone showed a certain truculence.

"Well they didn't get far with their experiments with their gas turbine engines did they?"

"Mmmhh..." Lance was non-committal.

"And they haven't done a great job with the Warships, have they?" The Warship diesels were notorious as failures; they were plagued with a whole range of problems. Swindon seemed incapable of getting them right.

Lance hauled his watch out of his fob and glanced at it. "Time to get over to the enginemen's hostel Harry, if we want any tea."

"You go on ahead, Lance," replied Harry, "I'm for a pint first; I'll see you later."

Harry walked off to the nearest pub to enjoy a private celebration; it was the very first time in five years he had won an argument with Lance Hargreaves. Harry Paisley was determined to savour the moment.

16 - Wedding bells for Lance and Sally (May 1961)

"You're going to be on with another driver for a couple of weeks, Harry," commented Driver Hargreaves to his fireman as they drew in to Leamington with a local passenger from Birmingham. "You'll need to be on your best behaviour, 'cause I'll be asking him how you went."

"Why, Lance? Summer holiday coming up?"

"Nope! I've got other plans."

"What other plans?" asked Harry curiously, "You're not training on the diesels, are you?" Harry patted the backhead of their Prairie 2-6-2T, "Not giving up on these already?"

"Ah well, I suppose I'll have to one day; but no, it's something much more satisfying than that." Lance lowered the regulator as they slowed and pulled up in Leamington Spa General station.

"If you're a very good boy and nip out and uncouple so we can run round for the return to Snow Hill, I'll tell you all about my plans." Harry shook his head in amusement but climbed down from the cab to disconnect the vacuum and steam heating hoses and lift the heavy coupling link off the hook of the first coach. He climbed back into the cab.

"Okay, what's the story?"

"Yours truly is getting married."

A smile split Harry's face. "When, exactly?"

Lance frowned at Harry's expression. "Next Sunday actually, why the grin?"

"I'm very happy for you," said Harry, his face all innocence.

Lance stared hard at Harry.

"That's not it," he said, "I know you; there's something else; come on, cough up; what is it?"

Harry chuckled. "Your wedding gets me five quid!"

"Five quid? What the hell are you talking about?"

"Lance, for months in Stafford Road there's been a book on you and Sally getting married. Some of the blokes said you wouldn't, some said you might in a year or two, an' I said this year!"

Lance was flabbergasted, but before he could respond, the ground signal clattered and they had to move forwards and over the crossover to back along the down main, crossing over again and coupling up to their five non-corridors once more. Harry dropped down to couple up and connect the two hoses before regaining the cab.

"You buggers!" began Lance, shaking his head and smiling ruefully, "You rotten buggers!"

"Look Lance, you can't expect the lads not to gossip about their mates. You and Sally have been living in sin for months, and any half-witted pillock can see that her lad is the spitting image of you."

"Yes, I see that, but..."

"And a few years back I met old George Denton, and he told me that since you'd met Sally, you'd almost stopped shagging practically anything else in a skirt."

"George never said that!"

"He bloody did! Mind you," admitted Harry, "He might have said it differently."

Their conversation interrupted by the guard's whistle, they concentrated on getting the train on the move back to Snow Hill.

Sunday's wedding was a fairly quiet affair and conducted in the small chapel near Lance's flat. Sally's parents from London were there, as was Lance's mother from her Chester old folk's home. Harry saw only a slight physical resemblance to Lance in his mother, but he smiled at the way she grabbed Lance's ear when she wanted to attract his attention; it was Lance to a 'T', as Harry well knew, having had his own ear seized in an identical manner on more than one occasion. But in fact most eyes were on Sally who looked 'very appetising indeed', as one of the Chester drivers put it. The light green dress set off her good looks and black hair perfectly.

"Pity you couldn't have done this a couple of years ago, Lance," whispered Ben Denton, "Dad would have really enjoyed seeing this; he had a soft spot for Sally."

Lance nodded sadly, "Yes, we shouldn't have waited so long, but he seemed so fit the last time I saw him. I had no idea how ill he was."

"No," sighed Ben, "He never let on to us either, but Mum's passing hit him harder than we thought."

The ceremony was simple but dignified, with the couple giving appropriate lip service to the rituals; neither Lance nor Sally accepted religious belief as an important feature of life, yet knew others did not always share this view and they were not inclined to give offence to them. They left the wedding breakfast early in the traditional manner, tin cans tied on to their hire car.

The next day at Wolverhampton's Stafford Road shed, Harry Paisley climbed into the cab of the Castle, ready to join another driver; he wondered at the appearance of the engine. It had been thoroughly cleaned and it shone in the sun as he began to oil the motion and check the gauges. They were to take *The Cornishman*, a Penzance train, as far as Bristol.

Harry had just checked the fire when he heard voices as the driver mounted the cab steps. He turned to see who his driver was to be and was astonished to see Lance, with young Billy, enter the cab.

"What the hell are you doing here – and in your driving gear?'

"Can't let you take this nice big engine all the way to Bristol on your tod, Harry; you might bend it."

"But, but..?"

"We're taking her as far as Bristol where we hand over to a Newton Abbot crew; then you and I part for a fortnight. Simple."

"And the lad here?"

"He's with us as far as Snow Hill, then he joins his mum in the train."

"Ah, I see; and will he be helping me with the firing?"

"One speck of dirt on him when he gets into the compartment and Sally will have my guts for a necktie!" Lance took the bag he was carrying and pulled out a cut-down overall. "Here Billy, put this on over your clothes or Mum will say a few rude words to me."

Billy laughed, "Like those words you said yesterday, when that man tipped his drink over your jacket, Uncle Lance?"

"Don't tell your mum about that, young Billy!"

Harry looked at Lance with one eyebrow raised in interrogation; "*Uncle?*"

"We're going to tell him in a few days, when he's got used to me being about all the time."

"Ah; well that makes sense," nodded Harry.

"Tell me about what, Uncle Lance?"

"My! Billy, what long ears you've got!"

Billy felt his ears, frowning. "They're not long!"

"They are sometimes! Now watch what Harry does with his big shovel."

Neatly distracted, Billy watched with interest as Harry placed his coal at various spots in the firebox, explaining to him about filling the holes in the fire. Pulling into Platform Four at Snow Hill, Lance said, "Right Billy, let's have that overall off you and I'll take you to your mum."

He climbed down and took Billy to where Sally was ensconced in a First Class compartment in the centre of the coach; here the vibrations from the rail joints rendered the ride smoother.

The relief driver and fireman at Temple Meads in Bristol stared at the Castle as it pulled in.

"Crikey!" said the fireman to his mate, "Look at that engine! They've done a real clean job of it in 'hampton; wonder why?"

Driver Jake Carson shook his head.

"Can't think why," he replied, "It might be one of the last times *The Cornishman* gets a steamer."

He noticed the crew waiting. "Hello Lance, haven't seen you for a while."

They exchanged details of the locomotive's performance and its load then Lance made his excuses, dropped down onto the platform and hurried away.

"Not like Lance," commented Jake to Harry in surprise, "He's usually pretty sociable… especially with women!"

He watched Lance walk along the platform to address an extremely attractive young mother with a little boy. "See what I mean? I bet he's going to try and pull that gorgeous bird with the little kid."

"Not quite," remarked Harry as he too climbed down the cab steps, "That gorgeous bird is his missus; they're on their honeymoon."
"Really? He's a lucky sod then, but taking on a girl who's already got someone else's kid takes guts as well."
"Have a good look at the little boy," invited Harry, pausing with a grin on the steps.
"What?" Jake stared at Billy and then at Lance. He laughed suddenly, "Oh yeah, I see what you mean."
He thought for a moment then and asked, "Is that why your engine's so clean? Have his mates at 'hampton done him proud?"
Harry's forehead creased as he considered, "I never thought of that; I did notice that the engine was unusually clean. He's very popular at Stafford Road, I bet you're right."

At Temple Meads Lance joined his wife in her First Class compartment (rather to the dismay of an elderly gentleman who looked with open disapproval at Lance's work clothes), picked up a bag and disappeared down the corridor from whence he reappeared a few moments later dressed in a jacket, flannel trousers and an open necked shirt.
"I feel more like a real honeymooner now," he told Sally as the old gentleman nodded in silent approval.
Leaving the train at Taunton, Lance, Sally and Billy waited for their connecting train to Minehead.
"Now Billy," Lance said as their train pulled in behind a small 2-6-2T tank engine, ' Look for a door which says 'First' because we're travelling first class today!"
Young Billy gazed out of the window as they ran through the Somerset countryside, and Lance pointed out various railway

features. Billy showed a sharp interest and an alert mind for a small boy, and Lance threw the occasional proud glance at Sally who smiled happily back at him. However, shortly after leaving Bishops Lydeard, the train stopped. Billy looked out of the window at the nearby signal. Lance and Sally were deep in conversation discussing plans for the next few days.

"Why have we stopped, Uncle Lance?" Billy asked.

"Probably a signal check," said Lance.

"No, the signal's pointing down; doesn't that mean it's clear?"

"Normally, yes," said Lance, "We'll move again in a moment or two."

However, after five minutes with no movement, Lance leaned out of the window. Billy was right, the signal showed 'clear' but there was no sign of any movement from the engine. Lance heard a shout and saw the train guard hurrying along the track towards the locomotive.

"What's up?" Lance called as the guard ran past.

"Don't know yet," puffed the guard.

"Keep an eye on Billy, Sal," muttered Lance quietly, "I think there's some emergency."

He opened the carriage door and, before she could stop him, dropped down to the track. Reaching the steps of the locomotive cab, Lance climbed up to see the fireman slumped in the corner and the driver and guard leaning over him.

"Anything I can do?" Lance asked, "I'm a driver on holiday. What's up with your fireman?"

"Dunno," said the driver worriedly, "He just keeled over five minutes back and hasn't moved much since. I can't get any sense out of him."

"You need to get him to a doctor, quick. Look, I'm a Western Region driver, I don't know this road but I do know locomotives. I'll fire for you and we can get to the nearest box and call for medical help. We could have a doctor waiting at the next stop."

The guard nodded, "If that's OK with you Ned, I'll authorise it."

"Fine by me," said the driver, relieved. He made his fireman more comfortable and the guard disappeared back to the rear of the train.

Ned watched as Lance took off his jacket and opened the firebox to examine the fire; he threw two shovels of coal accurately where they were needed and unwound the handbrake which had been wound on. He did all this smoothly and automatically and the driver realised that Lance knew what he was doing. The train moved gently away and stopped again a few minutes later at the next signal box.

"What's up, Ned?" the shout came from the signalman who was leaning out of his window, "You're running fifteen minutes late!"

Ned explained the situation and the bobby nodded. "Right! I'll call Jack at Williton, he'll call a doctor for you."

At Williton station, a young doctor was already waiting on the platform and he hurried up the cab steps and began to examine the comatose fireman.

"Hmm," he said, "We'll need to get him into an ambulance and into hospital. I'm not certain what the problem is, but I don't like his condition." Lance and the doctor lowered the fireman on to the platform where a porter had a stretcher waiting. The porter and the doctor carried the fireman on the stretcher into the waiting room while the stationmaster rang for an ambulance.

Meanwhile, Ned and Lance, having seen that the fireman was in safe hands, set to work once more to try and catch up some of the lost time. It was getting on for the summer season and this line served holiday resorts which were already beginning to fill up with holidaymakers. Any delays could affect the busy holiday timetable all over north Somerset.

As they ran into Watchet, Lance suddenly put down his shovel. "Shit!" he exclaimed, "I forgot to tell Sally, my missus! She'll be wondering where the hell I am."

There were quite a few passengers alighting at Watchet and as Ned was winding on the handbrake they heard a voice from the platform calling up, "If you've got those new trousers dirty, Lance Hargreaves, you'll be sleeping in the spare room tonight!"

Ned cackled. "You don't need to tell her, mate; I think she already knows!"

17 - The Great Freeze (December 1962)

The British Railways network was undergoing great changes. The regions had been 'rationalised', in the government's terms, in preparation for further great changes designed to make the system profitable, or at least less of a burden on the taxpayers.

The economists were drawing attention to the apparent huge costs of maintaining an efficient railway system compared to road transport where much of the cost could be transferred to private citizens or large commercial organisations. (There was little reference to how the Swiss were able to keep public transport profitable with a modern and effective system).

The British Government was planning to cut costs by closing two thirds of the system and by rapid withdrawal of all steam power in the remaining third. As a result, steam engine maintenance was gradually being run down and problem engines were now more likely to be placed on the scrap sidings as major repairs were no longer considered viable.

Many steam sheds were amalgamating and others were closing down or turning over to diesels only. Chester was typical: Western locomotives, previously using Chester WR shed were now serviced either at the London Midland shed or at Mold Junction on the North Wales line. Duties previously allocated to ex-GWR locomotives were being taken over by ex-LMS or BR engines or the new diesels. The regional boundaries had all been redrawn and most of the old Great Western main line from Paddington to Birkenhead had been transferred to the London Midland Region. After being a Western man all his working life, Lance was now an unhappy Midland man.

Bumping into Western colleagues in Paddington or Worcester, he was met with, "Where's yer red uniform, Lance?"

The influx of diesels was a mixed blessing; most steam locomen approved of the far cleaner and more comfortable working conditions and were only too glad to put their shovels and oil cans away for good. But the diesels were coming in far too quickly and with insufficient thought as to their design. Consequently they were often prone to breaking down, and most of the bigger steam sheds kept a few withdrawn steam engines for emergencies. The bigger diesels were taking over many of the express trains and the larger steam locomotives were sent into storage.

James Lofthouse the shedmaster spotted Lance coming in for his shift and called him over.

"I've got a sad duty especially for you, Lance," he said, "You're on the Paddington today with a King and 15 on."

Lance scratched his head, "What's so sad about that? I've done that often enough."

"When you bring her back here, she'll be withdrawn; and she's the last one."

"Ah!" Lance sighed and his face dropped, "Well it had to happen; Old Oak Common, Newton Abbot and Laira have already lost theirs, I hear."

"Yes, but she's not going for scrapping just yet; I'm keeping her handy in case we need her for emergencies; you never know with these diesels."

Lance nodded sadly; like all footplatemen, he had known that the days of steam locomotives were numbered, but unlike many he did not relish the idea of driving diesels and wanted to stay with steam as long as he could. He called into the enginemen's cab for his fireman and they walked over to their engine then climbed into the cab. The fitters had seen to it that the engine was in fine fettle, proper Welsh steam coal was piled in the tender and the cleaners had also been busy. The engine gleamed in the low December sun as Lance and Harry took her into Wolverhampton Low Level station to wait for the Birkenhead train to arrive. It came in on time and the ex-LMS Jubilee which had brought it from Chester was uncoupled for the King with its five extra coaches to be backed on. "Right Harry," said Lance "We're going to show them what a King can still do."

Harry nodded in approval; he was equally eager to show what this 35-year-old engine was capable of, especially since it had been improved only five years earlier. The Kings had all had front-end drafting improvements in the mid-1950s and had many years of life left in them, but with the diesels taking over, there was little work left for such powerful steam locomotives.

As Lance lifted the regulator, the locomotive moved off effortlessly and began to accelerate. It had to be held in check; the route between Wolverhampton and Birmingham Snow Hill was always busy and there was little chance of hard express running.

In Snow Hill the word must have got out that the Kings were being withdrawn as there were many photographers, young and old, on the platform to record the scene. Platform Four was its usual busy self with a London express but they got away again on time.

At Leamington Spa they noticed a down passenger waiting with a grimy Castle at its head and a Warship class diesel standing alongside. The Castle driver saw Lance and grinned, pointing at the diesel with his thumb down. Lance beamed back and, chuckling to Harry, said, "The down Wolverhampton's diesel has failed and been substituted by a Castle!"

The glee in his voice was unmistakable.

They kept good time to the next stop at Banbury, and then Harry was told to loosen his muscles for the run down the Chilterns to Paddington; this was going to be one for the books, explained Lance, if there were no hold-ups. Run they did. For once the line was clear, twice the speedometer touched 100 mph before they had to ease up past Acton but they still managed 85 again through Westbourne Park before smoothly coming to a stop four yards from the buffers at Paddington 12 minutes early.

Their return run on the 12.10am sleeper was less dramatic but once more the King showed that it wasn't ready for retirement, no matter what the accountants thought. It was past five in the morning before Lance got home, deeply saddened by the knowledge that he would never again be able to drive his favourite engines.

By late November, the weather had turned bitterly cold. Track maintenance was a nightmare for the platelayers who had to go out to deal with the frozen points and signals; parts of the system, particularly in the north, were even blocked by snowfalls and the snowploughs were kept busy.

At Wolverhampton Stafford Road shed, Lance was staring at the board, frowning.

"We're in for a bad time, Harry," he commented to his fireman, "We've got a slow freight this morning; 44 ten-tonners of coal from Salop to North Acton. We'll be sitting in sidings half the time; we'll have to keep the firebox open. You know what that means!"

"Yes," replied his fireman, "I do; I'll have my phiz on fire and my arse freezing."

"At least we've got a 38; if it's in reasonable nick it should do the job. We'll pull the tarp over us to keep some of the warmth in."

The 38 class 2-8-0 freight locomotives were strong and had slightly bigger cabs than the older 28 class engines, but they were usually paired with low tenders, which meant that the protection was more in the intent than in the effect. This was not a shift to look forward to. The weather had turned very cold and steam locomotive enginemen all over the country were suffering; no cabs had heating arrangements and in such extreme cold weather footplatemen opened the firebox doors or leaned on the backhead.

They waited at Salop for the train to arrive and relieved the half-frozen Birkenhead crew, who rapidly climbed down, muttering thankfully that they weren't brass monkeys, but that at least the engine was performing to their satisfaction even if the weather wasn't. But both Lance and Harry were already shivering by the time they passed Wellington. Matters weren't helped by the slow speed of the train.

"Pity we haven't got a tank engine with a local passenger," grumbled Harry, "We'd be warmer in an enclosed cab."

"True enough," agreed Lance, "But then some other poor sods would have to be in this."

"Yeah, I s'pose you've got a point there, Lance."

Shortly after Wolverhampton they were directed into a long refuge siding to allow an express past; but well after it had passed, the signal remained at danger.

"Nip over to the box, Harry, and ask the bobby how long we'll be stuck here in the Arctic," said Lance.

Harry climbed out and hurried to the signal box, waving his arms to create some warmth. He returned a few minutes later.

"We could be here for another half hour," he growled, "There's some problem up ahead."
"Time for a brew then," said Lance, "It'll warm us up a bit."

After they had finished their tea, both men took out newspapers to try and distract themselves from the vicious cold. Shortly, Harry noticed a small boy standing by the track.
"Hey kid, you'd be better off at home by the fire, wouldn't you?"
"I like trains," explained the kid.
Harry looked at Lance then looked back to the boy, "Well come up here and warm yourself, you'll freeze to death out there."
The lad was dressed in short pants and a jumper and climbed thankfully into the cab, where he stood in front of the open firebox to thaw himself out.
"Where's your overcoat?" asked Lance curiously.
"Got no overcoat," answered the lad, "Me dad's run off a year back and me mum can't afford no overcoat fer me nor me bruvver."
But for a lad who claimed to like trains, he showed very little interest in the workings of the cab as Harry tried to get his attention.
"Poor little sod's too bloody cold," muttered Harry aside to Lance, "Oh, let him get warm until we move off."
No-one spoke for a while and the youngster held his hands in front of the fire until the signal clanged down.
The lad looked gratefully at the enginemen and said, "Ta fer me warm 'ands."
He climbed down from the cab and scampered off.
Lance released the brakes and eased the train slowly over the points and back onto the main line once more. There were several

more hold-ups as they were shunted into sidings to let faster trains past, but by the time they reached Acton North yard, both men could hardly move; their heavy coats and gloves had stiffened so much from the cold they had to ask for help in the enginemen's cabin to get them off.

They suffered agonies as the warmth in the fug of the cabin began to reach their extremities. The door opened again and Jack Hibbert, their guard, came in; he too put his hands straight to the fire but he had a grin on his face.

"Who did you two have in your cab in that refuge south of 'hampton?" he asked.

"Just some kid who was standing by the track; poor little bugger was freezing with no overcoat. We had to take him in to warm him up," said Harry.

The guard looked at Lance, "Did Harry get your permission?"

Lance nodded, "I couldn't see any harm in it, Jack. We were stuck there for a while anyhow."

Lance wasn't worried; he knew the guard well and knew he wouldn't report the incident; "Why do you ask? Harry's right; the kid was shivering."

"He wouldn't have been shivering for long, you didn't see the kid's brother then?"

"No? Though he did mention his brother. Did you see him?"

Jack laughed out loud, "Yes, I saw him and his mate; while you two were doing your Good Samaritan act, one lad was in one of the wagons chucking lumps of coal out and the other was putting them into sacks. I saw them running away with enough coal to keep a house warm for a week!"

After the guard had gone, Lance shook his head in disappointment and said to Harry, "No matter how smart you think you are, there's always going to be someone smarter!"

Harry turned his face quickly away so that Lance wouldn't see his grin. He was deeply impressed; not many adults were able to outsmart his driver.

Yet Lance Hargreaves had been outwitted by three children.

18 - Lance begins to run out of steam (April 1963)

Like many Western drivers who found themselves in the cab of one of Sir William Stanier's 'Black Fives', Lance felt very much at home, even though it was a 'foreign' engine, as the ex-Western men regarded non-Western engines.

The Black Fives had been developed in 1935 as general purpose locomotives and were based on Stanier's experience with the Great Western Hall class, also a highly successful mixed traffic design. Stanier's Black Fives were almost universally liked as they could be found pretty much anywhere in the kingdom. They had proved themselves to be versatile, equally capable of handling express passenger trains as well as fast freight trains; they handled well and were generally popular among drivers. Nevertheless, Lance was not happy with his present locomotive; it was due for serious attention in Crewe Works and he was unimpressed with its performance on the semi-fast from Chester to Wolverhampton.

It should have been an easy run with nine corridors, but the engine had been making heavy weather and Harry had been swearing at the quality of the coal. It wasn't just the coal that was causing them grief, however; the engine itself was not behaving like a normal Black Five should. As a result, they were running 14 minutes late out of Shrewsbury.

Aside from the appearance of the engine (traces of heavy rust were apparent on the boiler, where the paint had worn thin), Lance suspected a build-up of ash in the smoke box, which would partly explain the poor draft. Engine maintenance had suffered since the decision to dieselise the system, and the abysmal pay for shed staff was not enticing men into the industry.

"Not much we can do about this engine, Harry," Lance was disappointed; he hated being late, even when it was not due to any fault of his own.

Harry put down his shovel and mopped his brow. "You're right there, Lance," he replied, "I'm knackered already, and we've only been on shift for three hours."

They were able to make up two minutes by the time they reached Wolverhampton and were thankful to uncouple and bring the engine into Stafford Road shed, where they sought out the shedmaster with their litany of complaints.

They were further soured to hear his views on the engine, "Sorry you don't like her, lads," he said, "Because when she's been turned and coaled, you're taking her back on a Snow Hill to Salop stopper."

"Well, it'll be Salop's problem then, won't it?"

"No Lance," interrupted Harry looking at the smoke-box shed plate, "6b – she's a Mold Junction engine."

Their engine was little better on the run to Shrewsbury but they persevered and brought their train in. The Salop shedmaster, when he heard of their complaint, after conferring with his Mold Junction colleague, decided to send the locomotive light engine to Crewe for urgent attention.

"Short run to Crewe, lads, and then back on the cushions to Wolverhampton High Level," he said breezily, "Easy peasy!"

Lance's muttered response was muted but indicated a lack of enthusiasm.

By the time they started out once more, the locomotive was in such bad shape that Lance said to Harry on reaching Wem, "We're not going to get as far as Crewe or even Nantwich, Harry. I'm going to fail her here or she'll be stuck on the main down somewhere between here and Whitchurch."

"I agree," Harry felt defeated, "Even without a train, I'm getting nowhere with her."

The stationmaster at Wem was unimpressed, but couldn't argue; the locomotive was shunted on to a siding in the yard and a report was sent to Crewe. Crewe North shed sent a Jinty 0-6-0T tank engine to tow the Black Five to Crewe. Lance and Harry caught a stopping train back to Salop and from thence another to Wolverhampton, thus ending a long and disappointing shift.

"Ah well, Lance." commiserated Harry, "You can't win 'em all! By the way, how's young Billy these days? Has he settled into his new school?"

Lance brightened up, "Yes, he seems to enjoy it; in fact he has settled into his new life with Sally and me very well."

"Good thing too."

Five days later, six very puzzled drivers sat in the enginemen's cabin with the shedmaster, who held six matches in his hand.

"You lot are the best of my steam drivers," he said, "And you enjoy the job. Most others are looking forward to getting into the diesels full time. As you know, the Kings were officially withdrawn last December, but I've kept one as an emergency locomotive for several months now. I'm sorry to say I've been instructed that she's to go to the scrapyard soon. I've also seen you all looking with lustful eyes at her every time you go past. However, she's got one more excursion coming up as a Special, and one of you will drive her. Hence the six matches."

He walked past the drivers, getting each to pick a match.

"Bugger!" muttered Lance as he held his match, then he saw what his neighbour had. "You jammy bastard, Reggie!"

Reggie held up the short match in triumph.

"Right, she's yours, Driver Watson," said the shedmaster, "Your run is next week and you can pick your fireman."

Lance nudged him quickly, "I'll fire for you if you like, Reg."

"Sorry Lance, no; I'll take my own fireman. Frank would be mortally insulted if I took anyone else. In any case," Reg laughed, "If I had you with me in the cab, you'd want to bloody drive and I'd be firing!"

"Ah well, no offence Reg," said Lance, leaning back, "It was worth a try."

Some three weeks later, Lance and Harry were to take a rake of empty wagons to Oxford and carry on from there with an unfitted freight to Reading West, where a Swindon crew would take over. Lance was unhappy again as he saw the locomotive assigned to the task; it was an ex-LMS 8F – an excellent freight locomotive in its day, but by this time sadly run down and urgently in need of maintenance, like most steam engines - and equally unlikely to get it. The coal too was substandard, seeming to consist of the scrapings from a coalyard that hadn't received a decent load for some time.

"Not looking too good today, Harry," commented Lance despondently as he began to fill in the details of the trip in the logbook.

Harry glanced briefly into the tender and agreed, "Yeah, looks like we're going to have a rough trip again."

But neither man complained for long; they were gradually getting used to rough trips on badly maintained engines. This was becoming the norm these days as steam was being slowly phased out. An increasing number of trains were hauled by diesels, and it must be admitted that many of the drivers were quite happy to come off shift with clean collars and having sat in a clean cab for their day's work. Not all were saddened by the approaching demise of the steam locomotive with its hard and dirty work and the need to spend up to an hour preparing the engine to do its job. A diesel took a fraction of the time.

Furthermore, the mechanical problems which so plagued the diesels in their early days were beginning to be overcome and the locomotives were generally spending less time in the repair facilities than previously although there was still clear evidence of *schadenfreude* when a diesel failed and had to be replaced or – even more delightful to the steam men - towed by a steam locomotive.

The diesels were beginning to get their own back however, as an increasing sight was the reverse, where a steamer had failed and was being 'assisted' by a diesel.

"I saw one of the new 'Westerns' on a Shrewsbury to Paddington express the other day, Lance," Harry was being kept busy with his shovel as they trundled through Snow Hill on the Up slow line.

"Oh yes?" Lance was enviously eyeing the driver of the County class 4-6-0 on the down platform; it was heading a Birkenhead express and would come off at Wolverhampton or Shrewsbury to be replaced by a Black Five in all likelihood as far as Chester, where an ex-LMS or BR standard 2-6-4T tank engine would take it to on to its destination at Woodside.

"Who's on the down Birkenhead?" asked Harry as he noticed where Lance was staring.

"Gerry Matheson, the lucky bugger," muttered Lance but nevertheless, he waved to Gerry as they passed.

Gerry looked out from his cab, saw Lance and his engine, and made a sympathetic gesture; Gerry too preferred ex-GWR engines.

"Those Westerns might be diesels, but I have to admit they look better than the rest," continued Harry.

"What? Oh yeah," Lance was not interested. He was more concerned with the state of their engine, which was beginning to demand more of his attention than he liked.

They trundled through Lapworth and Warwick before turning on to the Oxford line at Banbury, continuing through Oxford station where there was a heavy smog, requiring a slower speed than usual. They glimpsed the station buildings only dimly through the murk as they rumbled slowly through on the up main line through the station.

"Keep a sharp eye out for the signals, Harry," warned Lance, 'this is getting bad."

It was also getting unseasonably cold, and the two men were shivering in their cab.

As it was, they came close to overshooting Oxford's Hinksey Yard, only realising where they were as they reached the signals and points leading into the yard. However, once in the yard, things were no better; they drew their empty wagons into an arrival siding where they were uncoupled, but finding their unfitted freight to Reading West proved difficult.

The shunters who would normally guide them were having their own problems; nobody knew for certain what was where. Lance and Harry, who had hoped for a chance to rest and have a brew up, were equally frustrated. They were guided twice to the wrong siding before they finally coupled up to their unfitted goods. They were running an hour late already as they made their way back on to the up main. Yet here again progress was slow; the smog was getting thicker and they could not see far enough ahead to maintain any kind of speed. The only advantage was that Harry could see to the fire and had time to fill the holes in it. Lance was wondering whether to fail the engine when they reached Didcot where there was a large shed; here he could be sure of a replacement locomotive, but it might be a diesel. He decided to soldier on and try and coax the engine the last few miles to Reading and warn the Swindon crew of the problems.

In spite of Harry's efforts, not enough steam was reaching the cylinders, much of it was leaking from glands, steamchest joints and drain cocks before it could be put to good use. However, by dint of Harry's careful firing and Lance's experience, they were able to reach Reading West where the next crew was waiting for them. At least the smog was thinning slightly

"Sounds like you've been having problems, mate," said the Swindon driver, "How bad is it?"

"Bad enough," replied Lance, "You might have to think about failing her at Newbury or somewhere, but if the smog stays, at least you'll have the chance to build up the fire. Harry here's been very busy, but there's enough coal left still; you might make it."

The two men made their way back to Reading's main shed for a tea break and a return on a passenger train to Wolverhampton.

"Look on the bright side, Lance," said Harry in an attempt to cheer up his driver.

"What bright side's this then?" demanded Lance.

"What exactly didn't you like about this shift?"

"Mainly the lousy fire, the lousy steam leaks and the lousy cold in April, not to mention the fact that we're getting a lot of lousy engines these days. Apart from that, nothing much. Why?"

"Good thing we've got a compartment to ourselves; the passengers wouldn't like to hear their enginemen's lack of faith. And you didn't mention the lousy fog."

"Nothing you can do about fog, it's natural."

"Then we've nothing much to worry about, have we?"

"What the hell are you wittering on about?"

"Think about it, Lance," said Harry brightly, "Poor engines, poor fire, no steam tightness in the locomotive, cold cab."

"So?"

"In three years we'll be in diesels," chuckled Harry. He stood up and moved out of reach of Lance's fist, "No cold cabs, no fire to be fed, no steam leaks, and brand new locomotives – you won't know you're born!"

Harry slid the compartment door open and headed out. He just caught Lance's rejoinder, "No lousy firemen either!"

"Ouch!" Harry winced to himself as he walked along the swaying corridor to the toilet, "I walked smack into that one!"

19 - Decimation by the Doctor (October 1964)

It was rare to see an ex-GWR locomotive on a Paddington express; these were now often hauled from Chester by ex-LMS Jubilees, Black Fives or the BR equivalents. Even then, steam locomotives were frequently replaced at Shrewsbury or Wolverhampton by diesels for the rest of the run to Paddington. There were still ex-GWR locomotives to be seen at Oxford or Didcot and on the main line to the west, but they were usually in appalling condition and the named engines had often had their name - and even sometimes numberplates - removed to frustrate the souvenir hunters; numbers were chalked on.

The Kings had, of course, all gone. Many had already been scrapped but a few were still in the huge scrapyard at Barry. The class leader, *King George V*, had been sold to a cider company in Hereford. They were maintaining it in order - one day, they hoped, to break the proposed Western Region steam ban and run it once again. Their optimism was to be rewarded; the locomotive was to run again several years later and was so popular as to lead to widespread public enthusiasm for running withdrawn steam locomotives, and to encourage the re-opening of many closed routes as preserved railways, thus establishing a major tourist industry.

The name on all lips these days was that of Dr Richard Beeching, the government appointee whose job was to consider ways to reduce the huge financial burden on the railways of the United Kingdom. His conclusion was that a radical overhaul of the system needed to be undertaken; he proposed, amongst other things, a rapid withdrawal of all steam locomotives, a change to diesel and electric main line services, and indeed a closure of almost two thirds of the whole network. The ex-LMS main line to the north, now more commonly referred to as the West Coast Main Line, was already being electrified. Stanier's magnificent Pacific locomotives, designed expressly for this duty, were demoted to lesser roles such as the North Wales route and were rapidly being withdrawn. Like the ex-GWR Kings and Castles, there were still years of life but little work left in them.

In the enginemen's cabin at Wolverhampton's Oxley shed, the Stafford Road shed having been closed the previous year, Tom Leicester looked at the board and started laughing.
"Bad luck Hargreaves," he chortled, "They've given you a County for the Birkenhead; I've got a Black Five for the Worcester!" Tom was a relative newcomer to the Shed, having been transferred from Stoke, and had made himself quickly unpopular with his colleagues as he openly expressed pleasure at the misfortunes of others.
Lance smiled, "I can live with that; the Counties are perfect for the Chester run; they pull better even than Castles up the hills and get their breath back downhill again!"
Another engineman glanced at the board, "And you haven't got a Black Five, Leicester, yours is a BR Class five. I'd take a Stanier Black Five over a BR Five any day of the week!"
Tom Leicester merely grunted, picked up his lunch box and left the cabin.
The big Western 52-class diesel drew into Wolverhampton with the Down Birkenhead express; four coaches were uncoupled, leaving ten to be taken on to Chester by Lance and Harry in their County

class 4-6-0. This time, unusually, their engine had been well prepared and even polished, and they felt all the better for working in the clean cab.

"I'm surprised that we've got such a flash-looking engine, Lance," commented Harry as he lifted the firehole door to inspect the fire. "What's so special about this one?"

"Beats me," replied Lance, "But I don't like what I'm thinking!"

"Okay, what *are* you thinking?"

"I'm wondering whether this engine's on her last run."

"Her last run?" Harry was surprised, "Why? The Counties have only just been improved half a dozen years back!"

Lance nodded, "Of course they have, but tell that to the politicians who manage our railways! Since the end of the war the railways have been pretty largely ignored, and we're now paying the price! There's been little or no major maintenance, and no forethought. The silly buggers in government, Tory *and* Labour, have put most of their money into roads and sooner or later we're all going to regret that."

Lance was well into a pontificating role, "It'll be years before they realise it and then we're going to have traffic jams everywhere."

Harry stayed silent, he was not so sure that he agreed but with his driver in this mood, he didn't feel like arguing the toss. He concentrated on once more checking the gauges and the fire while waiting for the guard's green flag.

"OK Lance, we've got the green," he called out.

Lance released the brake and lifted the regulator gently. The locomotive moved off slowly and effortlessly.

Harry began placing a few shovelfuls around the firebox where holes were appearing, as Lance increased speed past Dunstall Park.

The undulating stretch had its varying gradients between Wolverhampton and the next stop at Wellington. The County took the rising gradients in its stride while Harry used the downhill runs to top up the fire and the boiler, and they pulled in to Wellington one minute early. This was fortunate, as porters unloaded cases and trunks from the brakevan as well as a number of boxes of pigeons for release later; this held up the departure for another minute, but the engine's ability to cope was once more shown as they arrived in Shrewsbury also a minute early.

The run between Shrewsbury and Chester was uneventful until they reached Ruabon; here a doctor had to be called as an elderly passenger was taken ill and needed to be transferred to hospital by ambulance.

Lance noted the loss of eight minutes in his driver's notebook and looked at his fireman.

"Get ready for some hard work, Harry," he said, "We've got eight minutes to try and regain!"

Harry grinned as he took up his shovel; he was looking forward to the run down Gresford Bank and the race across the Dee plain to Saltney Junction.

"Hope we get the signals in our favour," he replied as they left Wrexham. Running down past the collieries at Gresford, Harry built up the fire while Lance kept the train in firm control down the curves of the bank; but once down on the plain he opened up and let the locomotive have its head. There were no more stops until they reached Chester, and they picked up speed across the Dee valley, racing through Balderton until they slowed down for the run up to Saltney Junction where they joined the main London Midland tracks to North Wales. Lance maintained a steady pace through the cutting and across the Dee bridge before curving around the racecourse, under the City Walls and through the two tunnels into the General Station where he brought the train into a stop right on time.

Harry and Lance looked at each other and grinned.

"I'm really going to miss doing this," said Lance, "That was an exhilarating run!"

"But you could do that with a big diesel just as well," remarked Harry, playing devil's advocate.

"No you couldn't!" Lance's voice was adamant.

"Of course you could! Those big Western class diesels have got... what? 70,000 lb tractive effort; that's more than twice what this County's got."

"Your trouble, Harry, is that you've got no soul! The diesels have the speed and power, I grant you, but in a steamer, you've got the pounding of the rods, the smell of the steam, the beat, and fire and the open cab. A diesel's got none of that."

Harry nodded. "Yes, I'll grant you that, but you forgot something."

"What?"

"You forgot to mention the aching back from firing, the shaking floor of the cab when at speed, the frozen arse in winter, the oil on your hands and overalls every day, the hour spent in preparation..."

Harry dodged as Lance aimed a mock fist at his head.

On their return to Wolverhampton with the County later in the day, they were saddened to learn that Lance's earlier pessimism had been justified; the locomotive was withdrawn.

Its brass name-plates and number-plates were removed and it was shunted onto a siding ready to be towed with a couple of other dead locomotives to a scrapyard in Sheffield.

When booking on the next morning, Lance was called into the shedmaster's office.

"Can you guess what I've called you in for, Driver Hargreaves?"

The shedmaster sounded serious. Lance was puzzled; he hadn't, as far as he could recall, done anything to warrant this unusual formality.

"Er, no sir," he replied, but before the shedmaster could respond, there was a deep growl from outside as a Class 37 diesel eased past the door. The shedmaster pointed at it and for Lance the penny dropped. He nodded.

"You want me to start training on the diesels."

"Yes, Lance; I've put you down for next month's intake; I want you back on the London and Cardiff routes within six months."

Lance had known for some time that this was inevitable, but he hadn't anticipated the blow so early. The recent run with the County to Chester and back had been a real joy and the thought that he would never again have such an experience saddened him deeply.

"You're taking me off the steamers?" he enquired; the disappointment in his voice was obvious.

The shedmaster shook his head, "No Lance, we'll have them for at least another twelve months or so, but I want you ready for the final changeover."

This was a relief. Most of the other drivers were only too keen to get into the diesels; they saw it as much easier and cleaner work. The firemen, however, were more concerned; their jobs would be gone and unless they could transfer to diesel driving they might have to rethink their future careers.

For the next few months, Lance found himself busy learning how to drive a variety of diesels and what to do on the occasions when they broke down. His expressed pessimism on their reliability was, however, not reflected in the opinion of the diesel expert he spoke to at Swindon Works on a visit there.

"They've certainly been brought in without sufficient research and testing, Lance, I'll give you that," the engineer admitted, "But within a few years the early problems will have been sorted and they'll be no less reliable than the present steam locomotives. After all, they are rather more complex machines, so we must anticipate initial difficulties."

Lance nodded; this made good sense, but he still felt that he was losing the essence of his job as a driver. He had now been driving diesels for several months and had occasional conflicting emotions; the instant surge of power that a big diesel gave him on starting was nothing like that of a steam locomotive, and he enjoyed this at the same time as having a distinct sense of betrayal of his steam days.

He had to admit too that it was nice to climb into a closed cab on a day when in a steam locomotive he would have been wearing a heavy overcoat and gloves. Nevertheless, when he found himself in early April once more scheduled for a Birkenhead express with an ex-LMS Jubilee 4-6-0 at its head, he had a clear feeling of relief that he was back in familiar surroundings. As he climbed into the cab, he could forgive the locomotive for its failure to be an ex-GWR engine. In spite of its left-hand driving position, he felt instantly at home once more and the touch of his hand on the regulator was akin almost to a fondle rather than a firm grip. His only disappointment lay in the absence of Harry Paisley, his long-term fireman; Harry had been transferred to Didcot as a Passed Fireman and was now often driving. Lance's young fireman, Frank Hardman, seemed competent enough, but he was quiet and showed little enthusiasm for the job.

The run to Chester offered nothing more than the usual in the couple of hours that it took, and the return run an hour later with a BR Class Five 4-6-0 provided more of the same, but somehow the shift back into steam locomotives gave Lance an intense satisfaction, and as they booked off back in Oxley shed, he looked at his fireman, the youngster who'd had little to say during the shift.

"Now that today Frank was *real* driving!"

The fireman nodded; he had been firing long enough to appreciate the skill which Lance had demonstrated, and had shown his own competence on the right-hand side of the cab, but he had worked without any eagerness. He would be happy at being transferred to driving diesels when the time came. For him there was no magic of steam – it was hard and dirty work, and he would be glad when it was a thing of the past.

Lance sighed. Frank's attitude was that of so many of the footplatemen at Wolverhampton, and if the truth be told, of the majority of drivers and firemen in the country. Where had the days gone when men were proud of being engine drivers, and their jobs the ambition of so many boys? Interest in the job was generally low, as were the pay and the prospects.

Dr Beeching's reorganisation, it seemed, might impress the government accountants but it did nothing for the morale of the railwaymen.

20 – Lance reaches the BR terminus (Nov 1965 – Oct 1980)

Lance was not happy; he and Frank Hardman had run a loose fitted freight down to Oxford with a BR Class Four 4-6-0 in barely drivable condition. The run had been slow as the train had been backed into refuges several times to allow passenger trains through, and Lance had experienced great difficulty stopping and starting his train. Starting an unfitted freight without vacuum brakes was not a simple matter at the best of times; it had to be done with care as the wagons had to be gently brought into motion one by one to reduce the risk of breaking a coupling and parting the train. If the locomotive was not readily responsive to the regulator then the task became even more difficult. By the time they reached their destination in Oxford South Yard, Lance was soaking in sweat, in spite of the cold, and had employed most of the earthier range of his extensive vocabulary.

Even Fireman Hardman, not an enthusiastic steam man, was impressed by Lance's expert handling in a demanding situation with a poor tool. Only the previous week, Lance had taken the same freight with a Class 33 diesel, returning to its Southern Region base, and had found the duty a much less onerous undertaking. He was actually beginning to wonder whether the transfer to diesels was such a bad thing for the railways.

This view was strengthened on their arrival at Oxford. After a tea break in the enginemen's cabin, their return roster was on a local passenger to Birmingham Snow Hill. Their engine was a dilapidated Hall class 4-6-0 in appalling external condition; the engine had no nameplates and the number had been hastily chalked on the side of the cab. There were streaks of rust down the side of the boiler and the smokebox door showed clear signs of leakage. On climbing into the cab there was evidence that someone had attempted to improve matters; the various levers had been given a semblance of polish, the glass dials had been cleaned, the figures were more or less visible and the floor had been carefully swept.

However, in spite of its outward appearance, the engine seemed to be quite capable of handling its train and they had no trouble bringing it into Snow Hill, where an Oxford crew was ready to take the engine back to Didcot.

"I almost feel ashamed to be seen in engines like these," grumbled Lance to his fireman, "Even in the dark days towards the end of the last war our engines didn't look as grim as they do now."

Frank nodded sympathetically. Even though he much preferred to work in diesels, he appreciated Lance's driving skill and enjoyed the times with this obviously gifted driver. He knew, however, that his own career was linked to the new British Railways and its diesel fleet, although he actually wanted to transfer to the main line electrics some time in the future.

Lance Hargreaves knocked on the shedmaster's door and heard the familiar "Come in!"

He entered and the shedmaster looked up at him.

"Ah, Lance. Take a seat."

This was a serious matter; the shedmaster didn't offer seats unless there was something important to discuss. He shuffled among his papers and lifted out a letter.

"I have received a letter from our masters in Crewe. They state that steam will be completely phased out of BR by the end of 1968; the Western, as you know, will end next month."

This was not news to enginemen; they all knew that steam was on its way out, while wondering what the half-wits in government had been thinking about when building steam engines as late as 1960. Most footplatemen who had driven them knew the 200 9Fs were superb engines with a life expectancy of well over 20 years.

"The end for us in the London Midland Region will focus on the North West, and we've been offered a place for two experienced steam enginemen up in Preston. You're one of my best steam drivers; are you interested? I know they're not your Great Western engines, but most of them are Stanier's and the GWR taught him how to build engines!"

Lance smiled; this was true and the ex-LMS engines designed by William Stanier contained many features of GWR engines; his wonderful boilers were based on Churchward's tapered design. The versatile Black Fives were a modernised version of Collett's extremely successful Hall class mixed traffic engines, and Stanier's Princess Royal class express engines had been his variation on the GWR King theme; an engine whose design Stanier had been involved with.

Lance only took a moment to consider the offer.

"No sir, thanks," he replied. "I much prefer steam locomotives as you know, but I once made a mistake by moving and missing out on helping my family. My lad is happy at his school; the missus has a good local job, and, let's face it, I would only be driving steamers for a couple more years anyway. It's simply not worth the move."

"No, I thought that would be your view. I'll post the offer on the board and see if I can get any takers. I'll try and keep you on the few steamers we have left as long as I can, but you'll have to get onto the diesels from time to time as you've already retrained on them."

"Yessir," replied Lance sadly.

He had driven most of the diesel types, but he had been happy in steam cabs for almost 30 years. On the other hand, he found driving the diesels was not as bad as he had originally feared; they had their idiosyncrasies, as he was beginning to find out, but he was definitely becoming keener on the option of sitting in a warm dry cab when the weather was bad. Furthermore, the condition of most of the steam locomotives he was driving these days was usually poor, sometimes downright appalling. There were leaks everywhere and maintenance was only done in dire emergencies. The usual solution for a failed steam engine was to drive it to the nearest shed and park it on the scrap siding to remove its coupling and connecting rods. It could then be hauled away with one or two others to a scrapyard.

This sight, common enough in the mid 1960s, always saddened Lance, even when it concerned a group of 'foreign' engines passing through to the huge scrapyard at Barry in South Wales.

Over the next dozen years, Lance adapted to driving the diesels and found that there were distinct advantages in working comfort over his steam days. The problems which diesel drivers faced had rather more in common with steam drivers than he had expected. Signals Passed At Danger ('SPADs' to railwaymen) still generated reports, endless paperwork and complication. Incidents with passengers did not decrease; misunderstandings between shunters and drivers still

caused confusion in goods yards; inclement weather kept its capacity to delay services with concomitant public condemnation, and, much to Lance's surprise, the range of ability and enthusiasm for driving was much the same as it had been in steam days. Some drivers were keen and highly competent, some were average in both areas, and a few were downright lazy and irresponsible.
In short, not as much had changed as Lance had anticipated.

Returning home from a shift one afternoon in the early autumn of 1980, Lance flipped his cap on the hook in the hall just as Sally came out of the kitchen. She paused and looked at him critically for a moment.
"You're getting fat," she remarked.
Lance looked down at his stomach. True, his trousers *had* begun to feel a little tight. Lance made a non-committal grunt, grabbed the day's paper and dropped into his armchair. His GP had recently made a similar comment about him and had recommended exercise. You didn't get much exercise in the cab of a diesel locomotive though.
These thoughts occupied Lance for a few days until he had a long changeover break at Hereford. Here he paid a visit to a local cider producer which owned steam locomotives and ran them on public excursions.

At home a fortnight later, he announced that he was taking a few days off. He had been invited to join the crew of a steam special to Chester and back. He would be in the cab with the driver and fireman. It was a locomotive he knew very well, *King George V*, and Lance instantly felt at home in the cab.

Once well into the run he was permitted a stint on the shovel and was also allowed briefly to drive the locomotive. It was immediately clear to the two crewmen that there was nothing they could teach this older driver.

In Hereford, Locomotive Inspector Geoffrey Cardew entered the office of the cider company's locomotive shed where their steam locomotives were housed.

He stuck out his hand, "Geoff Cardew, come to see whether your driver today is up to scratch."

"Ah, Mr Cardew. Thank you for coming early. My name is Jock Robertson and I am looking after the railway side of things here. We have a new man who wishes to join our list of available crews and we wanted you to watch him today and give us your written confirmation that he is fit to drive our engines, but the train has already left with him in it as an observer."

Geoff Cardew asked, "Who is he? I might know him."

"The new man is a Mr L. Hargreaves. He was at Chester and Wolverhampton before he transferred to the diesels. He then went to Swindon and…" He paused as Geoff started to laugh, "What's so funny?"

"Where's that confirmation document you need me to sign?" asked Geoff.

The form was handed over and Geoff took a pen from his pocket. At the bottom of the form he wrote, 'T*he above mentioned driver is fully competent to handle the duties of a steam locomotive driver.*'

Geoff signed his name with a flourish.

"You can't do that, Mr Cardew!" the official was aghast, "You haven't even seen him drive!"

"Oh but I have!" Geoff asserted emphatically, "I started firing in Chester and Lance Hargreaves was my regular driver for several years. He taught *me* to drive and he was one of the best drivers in the whole division. There's nothing he didn't know about driving steam locomotives. He transferred to Wolverhampton so that he could get his hands on the Kings. I still saw him a few times as our paths crossed. He gave me a couple of valuable tips the day before my Driver's test, and I passed first time. Shortly after that I transferred to the Worcester Division and we lost contact."

"Even so," said the official, "You don't know whether he can still drive – he must have stopped driving steam locomotives over a dozen years back."

Geoff Cardew shook his head.

"Take it from me; driving a steamer is not something you forget. I gave up steam in '65 when I went on to diesels, but by 1972 I was back on steamers working for some of the tourist railways in my spare time and have been employed since 1975, instructing and testing steam drivers on a full-time basis. Lance Hargreaves was the best driver I ever met – er – with one exception; that was old George Denton. George was Lance's driver right through the war. George and Lance were a cracking team and George made sure that Lance knew how to drive. Watching those two in action was an eye-opener. It was uncanny how each knew what the other needed. No," Geoff continued, "You need have no fear about Lance Hargreaves' driving."

Lance lay down his paper at breakfast one morning.
"Would you take it amiss, Love, if I were to retire from British

Railways?" he asked his wife.

Sally looked surprised, then said, "Of course not, Lance; we have enough to live on and Bill has his own job now, he doesn't need our financial support any more."

She mused further, "We could then make that move to South Devon we've talked about."

"My next point," continued Lance, "I need to get my weight down and need more exercise…"

"Yes indeed," interrupted Sally eagerly, "Walking along the cliffs and up around Dartmoor; very good for you."

"Er, not exactly what I had in mind," admitted Lance.

"What then?"

"There are a couple of tourist steam railways there looking for engine crews, and…" he stopped as Sally laughed and threw the tea cosy at him.

Some months later, Sally and Lance had bought a small cottage just outside Torquay. Sally rejoiced in dealing with the hitherto neglected garden and Lance found himself fully occupied working for the local tourist railway. He was soon driving small tank engines, Manors, and larger visiting engines. One evening after a shift, his grinning appearance back at home in greasy overalls and oily hands did not disturb Sally in the least. She had a half smile on her face.

"What?" demanded Lance.

Sally just shook her head.

"Nothing," she replied.

But it wasn't nothing at all. It was very important to her; her husband was a happy man once more.

The Engines

Steam locomotives were classified according to their wheel arrangements: the basis was the number of wheels used for driving, with other numbers used for small guiding wheels at the front and rear trailing wheels.

For instance, a 4-6-2 had a set of four small wheels in front of the drivers, to guide the engine around curves, six main driving wheels, and another set of two wheels at the rear to help take the weight. An 0-6-0 had only six driving wheels and no others; a T indicated a tank engine.

Engines were also classed according to their purpose, e.g. express passenger, heavy freight, mixed traffic (i.e. passenger or freight), or shunting.

Locomotives of the same design were also grouped under the name of the design.

GWR/Western Region

King class: The premier express passenger engine of the company. It handled all the heaviest express passenger trains from Paddington to either Plymouth or Wolverhampton. The 4-6-0s were restricted to these routes because of their great weight. Visually very similar to Castles.

Castle class: The largest class of express passenger locomotives. They were strong and fast 4-6-0s.

Star class: 4-6-0s and precursors to the Castle class. Strong and powerful and generally popular with their crews, but by the 1940s they were wearing out. Known as 'Forties' due to their numbers beginning 40xx.

Saint class: Similar to the Star class but with only two, not four, cylinders. Not quite so strong. These 4-6-0s were known as '29s'.

Hall class: These were extremely useful 4-6-0 general purpose locomotives and were found on most main routes of the Company's system.

County class: These were heavy general purpose 4-6-0 locomotives but were only built at the end of World War II. Initially not popular with many enginemen, but when modified they became very suited to hilly main lines.

Grange class: Another 4-6-0 general purpose engine, lighter and with smaller wheels, slightly more powerful than the Halls.

Manor class: Light 4-6-0 general purpose engines. Initially, as with the Counties, not successful, but once modified they became excellent engines for more lightly-laid routes.

Bulldog class: An early class of 4-4-0 general purpose engines with outside frames which made them appear obsolete, but in fact they were useful little engines.

47xx: Heavy 2-8-0 express freight locomotive occasionally used on passenger trains.

28xx: Heavy 2-8-0 standard freight locomotive.

Aberdare: Elderly 2-6-0 freight locomotives, mostly due for scrapping but kept on during World War II.

Mogul: Mixed traffic 2-6-0 locomotives. Known as the 43xx class.

Prairie: Mixed traffic 2-6-2T tank locomotives.

Pannier: Light 0-6-0T tank engines with square tanks on either side of the boiler.

Other companies' engines

LMS/London Midland Region

Duchess: Large 4-6-2 (Pacific) locomotives for heavy express work. Some were originally streamlined but this feature was later removed for ease of maintenance.

Royal Scot class: Express passenger 4-6-0 locomotives corresponding roughly to the Castles of the GWR. They were completely rebuilt in the 1940s and 1950s.

Patriot class: Medium-powered 4-6-0s for express passenger and parcels trains.

Black Five class: A medium-powered general purpose 4-6-0 and popular with enginemen as they were extremely versatile. They were Stanier's LMS version of the GWR 'Hall' class.

Jinty: Small 0-6-0T general purpose and shunting engine.

Glossary

For those less familiar with a few of the terms used by railwaymen of the twentieth century.

Banker: Extra engine used at the back of a train to assist it uphill.
Bay platform: Platform with a buffer stop at one end.
Blow-back: Rare burst of fire into the cab.
Bobby: Signalman.
Bogies: Railway term for coaches. Also a set of four or six wheels in a frame.
Brake van: Small van at the end of a goods train from which the guard could apply a brake to assist the driver when slowing the train. In a passenger train, the brake van would be a coach with a section for the guard.
Bushes: The thicker metal areas around the holes through which the coupling and connecting rods were attached to the wheels.
Big ends: The wider ends of the tapered connecting rods where they were attached to the driving wheel; the narrow ends were attached to the shaft into the cylinder.
Cleaner: Apprentice engine cleaner preparing to become first a fireman then later a driver.
Clinker: Partly-burned coal remnants which would stick to the grate and needed to be removed to allow air through the fire to aid combustion.
Corridors: Railway term for coaches used in longer-distance trains. They had corridors with toilets, as opposed to the non-corridor trains used for short distances.

Clear: A signal which indicates that the route ahead is clear for a train to proceed.
Control: The department of the railway company responsible for managing crewing of trains.
Detonators: Small explosive devices placed on the track to warn approaching trains in an emergency. On hearing detonators, a driver would stop immediately.
Distant signal: The signal giving warning of the status of the next section of track but one. Normally yellow with a black chevron stripe.
Down: The route direction away from London (see also 'Up').
Driver: The man responsible for driving the locomotive.
Empty Coaching Stock (ECS): A train of empty coaches to be taken where they were needed. These trains were not advertised in the public timetables and did not carry passengers.
Firebox: The section of the locomotive immediately in front of the cab, in which the fire would be situated.
Fireman: The man responsible for keeping the fire at a level sufficient to maintain enough steam for the driver to drive.
Fitted goods: A goods train fitted with vacuum brakes, which would allow it to travel at higher speeds than an unfitted goods.
Fouling point: The point in a siding at which a stabled train is clear of the main line.
Ganger: A member of a team whose job it was to check and maintain the safe condition of the railway trackwork.
Guard: The man in charge of a train. He travelled in the brake van at the rear of a goods train or passenger train.
Headshunt: Extra siding to allow a locomotive to wait before backing onto a train or to permit a shunting operation without

interfering with station or yard approach tracks.

Home signal: The signal controlling the next section of track. Normally red with a white stripe.

Hot box: Hot axle box of a vehicle filled with grease or oil; if it got too hot it could start a fire.

Injector: Pump in a steam locomotive to force water into the boiler.

Knocker up: A cleaner who would be used to wake up enginemen when they were needed on shift.

Light engine: An engine without a train.

Loose coupled: A train of goods vehicles fitted only with metal couplings and thus limited to a speed of 40 mph.

Loop: Side track to allow a train to be marshalled for departure or after arrival without blocking the main line.

Main: Tracks for fast trains.

Metals: Rails or tracks.

Non-corridors: Coaches used in short distance trains did not normally have their compartments connected by corridors.

Passed Cleaner/Fireman: Cleaner or fireman who had satisfied the authorities that he could be trained for promotion to the next rank. He could be used as a fireman/driver under training.

Pilot engine: Engine which would be added in front of a train engine and used to assist with a heavy train.

Plug: A fusible lead plug in the boiler which would melt if the water level sank too low, thus releasing steam pressure to prevent the boiler from exploding.

Regulator: Large lever in the cab of locomotives, enabling the driver to regulate the flow of steam to the cylinders, essentially controlling the speed of the train.

Semi-fast: Passenger train which does not stop at all stations.
Shed: Depot for steam locomotives, which were allotted to a particular shed for their day-to-day maintenance.
Shedmaster: Foreman in charge of a shed.
Shocvan: Goods van with special springs to prevent damage during shunting.
Siding: Stretch of track used to store vehicles until they were required.
Signalling: Used to control the movement of trains. A 'home' signal controlled the entry to a section. If it showed 'clear', entry was permitted. If it showed 'danger', entry was not permitted.
A 'distant' signal warned of the position of the next home signal; a 'clear' meant that the next home signal was also clear, whereas a 'danger' meant that the next home signal showed danger also and that the driver should prepare to stop his train at the next signal.
Slow: Tracks for slow/stopping trains.
Sole and heel: Light maintenance and repair to a locomotive.
Special: Non-timetabled train for a special purpose.
Steam heating: Most passenger trains had their coaches heated by steam pipes throughout the train.
Steam lance: Hose which could be connected to the boiler of a locomotive to force superheated steam through the boiler tubes to clear them of any blockages.
Steam pressure: The pressure of steam in the locomotive boiler.
Stopper: Passenger train which stops at most or all stations on its route.
Tank engine: Locomotive incorporating a bunker for coal and tanks for water; used for short-distance work. Could travel either smokebox- or bunker-first so did not need to turn on a turntable.

Tender: Special vehicle attached behind a steam locomotive to carry the coal and water needed.
35-tonners: Railway term for coaches. Thirty five tons was the standard weight of most coaches.
Unfitted goods: Goods train in which the vehicles are not fitted with vacuum brakes. See also 'loose coupled'.
Up: The route direction towards London.
Water troughs: Long metal troughs filled with water between the rails to allow locomotives to pick up water at speed.
Wheel tapper: Metallurgy expert who tapped the wheels of vehicles with a special hammer to listen for metal fatigue.

Common abbreviations

CLC: Cheshire Lines Committee; a small private railway company in Lancashire and Cheshire serving Liverpool, Manchester and Chester. HQ at Liverpool Central.
ECS: Empty Coaching Stock
GWR: Great Western Railway; a private railway company serving the West of England, South Wales and north as far as Birkenhead and Warrington. HQ at Paddington.
LMS: London, Midland and Scottish Railway; serving western and central England, the north-west and Scotland. HQ at Euston.
LNER: London and North Eastern Railway; serving eastern and north-eastern England and Scotland. HQ at King's Cross.
LT: London Transport; the authority for most Public transport in London, the Underground, buses, and trams.
SR: Southern Railway; serving southern and south-western England. HQ at Waterloo.

Acknowledgements

Once more, I must gratefully acknowledge the advice given to me by those whose technical railway knowledge surpasses mine. Dr John Ritter's assistance has been invaluable as he has again cast his eagle eye over the text in great detail. Further useful comments have been given by Ian Norman, Richard Davidson and Paul Brown all from the model railway fraternity here in Melbourne.

This time I have had the assistance of ex-railwaymen: Graeme Speers and Ron Stockton have both provided material in the stories, and Richard Antliff of the Great Western Society has also added helpful remarks and Michael Poole has provided a beautiful photograph for the front cover.

I am once more particularly indebted to Katharine Smith of Heddon Publishing who has given the book her expert editorial know-how. To all these friends I offer my gratitude, but none of this would have come to fruition if my wife Christa hadn't given me her constant moral support.

If you have enjoyed this book, we would be very grateful if you would take the time to review it on the Amazon website. A positive review is invaluable and will be greatly appreciated by the author.

Please also visit the Heddon Publishing website to find out about our other titles: www.heddonpublishing.com

Heddon Publishing was established in 2012 and is a publishing house with a difference. We work with independent authors to get their work out into the real world, by-passing the traditional slog through 'slush piles'.

Please contact us by email in the first instance to find out more: enquiries@heddonpublishing.com

Like us on Facebook and receive all our news at: www.facebook.com/heddonpublishing

Join our mailing list by emailing: mailinglist@heddonpublishing.com

Follow us on Twitter: @PublishHeddon

Printed in Great Britain
by Amazon